The Human Element: A Non-Technical Guide to Working with AI

Transform Your Career Using the Skills You Already Have

Eroll Chimanga

Contents

Part 1: Foundation and Mindset

Chapter One

Embracing the AI Revolution

Understanding Your AI Anxiety

Surely you remember how you felt when you first saw smartphones? Do you remember when they were a bit complicated—or maybe a little unnecessary? It's hard to imagine life without one now, right? Technology evolves in a fairly simple way: The internet changed how we receive information, electronic devices changed how we communicate, the cloud changed how we save information & share data, and today AI is changing the way we work and think.

When was the last time any news story about AI didn't make you cringe? Maybe it was about AI writing better marketing text than humans, handling better customer service than your team, or making financial predictions faster than your analysts.

Do you think it's been too long to start using AI? Or that you are too far behind the curve? Breathe. If you're a marketing manager, an HR professional, or a business analyst and you're impressed by how fast AI can create content or by how ChatGPT processes numbers faster than Excel, I understand how you feel. Do you find yourself fascinated but worried? It is normal and it matters a lot.

The Truth About AI and Your Job

Here's something important that you might not find in other books: It's not the AI itself that will replace your job; it's the person who knows how to use AI effectively who will outshine you. This is not meant to scare you; it is meant to empower you. Unlike what some may suggest, I am not going to try to "overcome" or "eliminate" your anxiety. Instead, I will take a different approach: I will make it your competitive advantage.

Your Doubts About AI Can Be a Superpower

Interestingly, those that are a bit sceptical about AI tend to do a better job than those who are gung ho and jump in immediately. What is the reason? They focus on the important questions:

- "But how will this really work in everyday situations?"

- "What are the possible issues in this situation?"

- "What impact will this have on our customers?"

- "What are we not considering?"

These are not just anxious thoughts; they are the key questions that make sure AI projects succeed. While many people are eager to put everything into action, you are considering the

The New Reality of AI Experience

Let's tackle the elephant in the room: yes, companies are asking for AI experience. But here's what most people don't realise—you probably already have more AI experience than you think.

Think about your phone. You're already using AI when you:

- Get email suggestions for responses

- Use face recognition to unlock your device

- Have your photos automatically organised

- Get traffic-aware directions

That's all AI. You're not just using it; you're adapting to it, evaluating it, and making decisions about when to trust it. That's a valuable experience.

Being Real with AI

Here's something refreshing, you don't need to pretend you're an AI expert. In fact, being authentic about your AI journey can be your strength. When you're learning to work with AI tools, treat them like a collaborative partner. Share your actual challenges, be specific about your goals, and don't be afraid to admit what you don't know. This vulnerability often leads to better results than pretending you have all the answers.

A Simple Way to Start

Let's do something practical. Grab a piece of paper (yes, go and get one—this works better than just thinking about it). Write down your three biggest worries about AI in your field. Be specific. Instead of "AI will replace jobs," write something like "I'm worried AI will make my financial analysis skills obsolete."

For each worry, write down:

- The human skill that makes you aware of this potential problem

- A real situation where this awareness could help in an AI project

- One question you'd want answered before implementing AI in this area

This isn't just a feel-good exercise; you're actually building the beginning of your AI professional toolkit. Those questions you're writing? They're the same ones AI project managers need to ask. Those concerns you're highlighting? They're the insights that AI teams are desperately searching for.

Moving Forward: Your New AI Guide

Think of your anxiety as a guide, not a barrier. It identifies areas where human understanding is needed for AI development. And while many are learning programming languages, you are learning something just as important: practical experience and understanding of people that AI cannot replicate.

You start your trip into AI without forgetting what you already know or ignoring your worries. The first step is to realise that your unique human point of view, complete with your worries, might be just what the AI business needs right now.

Remember that the aim is to not be just like AI. The aim is to be 100% genuinely human in an environment where AI takes care of the everyday chores. How about that journey? It begins with recognising your natural responses with regards to this evolution in technology.

Before we continue, think about this: What if your worries about AI are not a barrier but rather steering you to discover your own unique role in the field?

In the next section, we will start to look at how to turn your worries into professional opportunities. More importantly, I will aim to guide you in discovering your cause—your "why," which will significantly impact your AI journey.

***

Turning Fear into Opportunity

Do you remember the worries you noted in the previous section? Let's change them into something powerful using a method I call the Four E's of AI Opportunity. First, let's make something clear.

A Brief Note on AI Tools

When "AI" is mentioned in this book, I'm not talking about a technology that is far away in the future. I'm talking about tools that are already available for everyone to use right now. Here are some of the most popular ones:

- **ChatGPT**: Is your intelligent conversation partner for writing, analysis, and problem-solving

- **Google Gemini**: Very strong with real-time information and research

- **Claude** by Anthropic: Excellent for longer, more detailed analysis and complex tasks

- **Microsoft Copilot**: Is seamlessly integrated with Microsoft Office tools for daily work support

Important Note: The AI landscape changes rapidly. These tools will probably keep being essential, but their capabilities and features might have improved by the time you read this. Make sure you check the latest versions and features of these tools. The ideas and methods we go through will be helpful, whatever tools you choose to use.

Imagine these AI tools as handy assistants that can do things for you but still need your direction and knowledge. Not all of the tools are needed. Actually, starting with just one will let you use some of the strategies we discuss.

The Four E's: Your Framework for Success

1. Efficiency: Creating Space for What's Important

Do you remember that old saying about working smarter, not harder?? That will be our starting point. But here's what most books miss: AI-powered success isn't about accelerating work. It's about giving space to things that need human attention.

Real-world Example: Imagine you work in marketing and spend hours summarising customer feedback each week. Instead of reading the customer notes one at a time, Claude can sort response threads and highlight key patterns so you can focus on strategic responses. Use Microsoft Copilot to automatically summarise your Zoom or Teams meetings. It collects action items for when you're focused on the conversation.

2. Effectiveness: Make a Bigger Difference

This is where it becomes interesting. After you make that space by being efficient, you can concentrate on being more effective.

Real-world Example: If you work in sales, try using Google Gemini to look at industry trends and combine it with ChatGPT to find patterns in your successful deals. These tools can help you find the best time to contact and connect with different customers and recommend the best personalised techniques based on what has and hasn't worked for you in the past.

3. Empowerment: Taking Charge, Shaping Your Future

This might be the most exciting part. These tools act like your personal boosts:

Real-world Examples:

- Start a continuous conversation in Claude to talk about and improve your business ideas regularly.

- Use Google Gemini to keep up to date within your industry by having it review and summarise all the latest news and trends.

- Use Microsoft Copilot to turn your basic presentation notes into smooth PowerPoint slides.

- Keep a "Communication Coach" thread in ChatGPT to practice and improve important messages before you send them, be it internal or external.

4. Experimentation: A Comfortable Place to Improve

The last E is about allowing yourself to explore new things in a safe space.

Real-world Examples:

- Use Claude for role playing practice having difficult conversations by playing out different situations and responding to those situations

- Look for new ways of working with Google Gemini, it is possible to find possible problems by looking at similar cases.

- Create different versions of your project proposal with ChatGPT.

- Explore different methods to present data in your reports using Microsoft Copilot.

Finding Your "Why": The Missing Piece

There's an important point that many AI career books overlook: before you start learning how to use these tools, it's important to understand the reasons for learning how to use these tools. This isn't just about your job promotion. It's also about finding out what's important to you.

Think about this:

- What issues in your industry worry you the most?

- What challenges in your field seem to be impossible to solve?

- What changes would you like to see in your field?

The answers to these questions are where you begin. AI tools are simply tools. What matters is what you want to achieve with them.

Creating Your AI Help System

Getting the best results from using AI tools is not something you do alone. It's like learning a new language—you don't just practice on your own but need people to talk to, to check your pronunciations, etc., guides to help you, and in some respects, a group setting of others who are also learning helps. Here's how to create yours:

1. Start Where You Are:

- You can be sure that there are people in your company who are equally as inquisitive about AI, so find the "AI Champions" - people that are already using tools like ChatGPT or Google Gemini.

- Join online groups such as the ChatGPT subreddit or LinkedIn communities that focus on AI in your field or AI in general.

- Share what you learn by starting a straightforward "Today I learnt" document. In it, write down helpful AI prompts or interesting findings.

2. Create Learning Partnerships:

- Find a coworker to look into different AI tools together—you could focus on ChatGPT, and they look at Google Gemini, then share what you learn.

- Make a document that lists productive prompts and examples of how they are used.

- Plan regular meetings to explore AI tools together and then try them out.

3. Build Your Professional Network:

- Connect with AI experts on LinkedIn who have easy-to-understand, practical insights.

- Join groups for AI tools that you want to learn about.

- Join webinars and online events that focus on AI in your field.

- Share your view on how these tools can help with real business issues.

The Reality Check: Your Human Edge

What's interesting is that organisations are finding out that their main challenges with AI aren't about technology—they're about people. They are having a hard time with:

- Helping teams use tools like ChatGPT well

- Making sure AI solutions really address real issues

- Ensuring that automated processes still feel personal and have that human touch

A marketing team might use Microsoft Copilot for creating content, but deciding which content needs AI help and which should be made by humans requires your judgement and expertise.

Your New Work Journey

From today, think about changing how you see your role with AI tools:

- If you're concerned about AI tools making mistakes, try to think of it differently: You are the expert in quality control who understands what to look for and when to rely on the AI results.

- When you wonder how teams will cope with tools like Claude or Google Gemini, you show important awareness of change management.

- When you talk about the ethical issues of using AI, you're showing important skills in managing risks.

The Role of a Bridge Builder

Imagine putting AI into action like you were building a bridge:

- Teams understand how to use AI tools together

- Business leaders understand the results they aim for.

- How about you? You get that these tools should be designed and ultimately work to help people in their daily lives.

For example, when your company wants to use AI tools to provide customer service. You are the person who understands:

- Some customer interactions require a personal human touch

- How to combine ChatGPT's help with human knowledge

- When to get human assistance from AI support

Moving Forward

As we proceed to Chapter 2, you'll find something that may surprise you: the "traditional" skills you've built throughout your career are not going away. They are becoming more valuable because they show you when and how to use AI tools effectively.

It's important to note that AI tools like ChatGPT, Claude, and Google Gemini are just that: tools. Just like Microsoft Excel hasn't taken away the need for financial analysts. It's simply made them work much better with such a tool. These AI tools will not reduce the need for human skills but will make them stronger.

Think about this: What if all the things you've been anxious about losing, from an AI perspective, are exactly what the AI revolution requires the most?

In Chapter 2, we will look at how the skills you have right now give you a special edge in the world of AI. We will explore how to bring together your skills and AI tools to create value that neither can do on its own.

Remember: The AI tools that have been and will continue to be mentioned will likely evolve, but the principles of combining human expertise with AI help will be useful. Keep looking for new tools as they become available, but focus on the main strategies instead of the specific features.

Chapter Two

The Power of Non-Technical Skills in AI

Why Human Skills Are More Important Than Ever

Do you remember how we finished Chapter 1, thinking about whether the things you're anxious about losing could actually be what the AI revolution really needs? Here's some good news: you were likely already building your most important skills for the AI era without even knowing it.

The Big AI Puzzle

What's interesting is how AI tools like ChatGPT, Claude, and Gemini are getting better at managing technical tasks. Human skills are becoming more important, not less. It's like what happened in mathematics when calculators became widely used: all of a sudden, knowing what to calculate mattered more than actually doing the calculations yourself.

This contradiction is especially clear in the way work is evolving. Consider accounting, for example. As AI takes care of calculations and basic bookkeeping, accountants are now focusing more on giving strategic advice and planning for the business—tasks that need human insight and experience. In customer service, as AI takes care of simple questions, customer service agents are becoming more important for their skills in dealing with complicated situations that need understanding and creative problem-solving solutions.

The comparison of calculators is more than maths. Just as calculators let mathematicians focus on understanding difficult problems instead of calculations, AI tools are allowing professionals to focus on parts of their work that need human skills.

Note: The AI tools mentioned in this chapter evolve rapidly. While specific features may change, the core principles of how human skills complement AI capabilities remain constant. Focus on understanding these fundamental relationships rather than specific tool features.

The Changing Role of Human Judgement

A GPS system like the one on a phone like Google Maps can discover the fastest way to your destination, but it can't look at risks such as driving in an unsafe area. That's why human judgement is important even as we become more dependent on AI.

This happens in all kinds of jobs, from office workers to skilled trades to service providers. Here are a few examples from everyday life:

A hairstylist can use ChatGPT to get new style ideas or to improve service descriptions for their website, but a person has to decide which styles will work for a client's face shape, lifestyle, and personality. AI can suggest popular hairstyles, but when your client says, "dramatic change," they really just mean "a little trim."

AI tools like Claude can assist teachers in coming up with lesson plan ideas and making worksheets. However, it's important for teachers to use their judgement to recognise when a student is having difficulties not just with the content but also with personal issues that might be impacting their studies. AI can mark and grade papers, but you can tell when a usually enthusiastic student appears uninterested.

In small retail shops, Microsoft Copilot can help improve inventory orders using sales data. But owners will still have to use their personal judgement to understand if local festivals next month will increase demand. Or might this winter be different from last year?

A nurse can use AI tools to assist with patient paperwork or to quickly check for medication communications, but it's their human judgement that picks up on small changes in a patient's condition or understands when family issues are impacting treatment.

Emotional Intelligence: A Skill That AI Can't Copy

It's becoming clearer every day that as AI takes on more standard tasks, emotional intelligence is turning into a key skill for careers. Why is that? AI can handle emotions, but it doesn't really understand them or respond in a genuine way.

Let's look at a customer service representative at a nearby bakery. AI will help you write a good apology email if a wedding cake order is wrong or incorrect. But first, an individual needs to know how to recognise the bride's stress and how to handle the situation correctly. For a personal trainer, AI may create the perfect workout plan, but the trainer's ability to connect with the client tells them whether they need support or need a more aggressive approach.

A school counsellor can use AI to manage pupil files and to monitor ways of intervention, but it is their ability to understand emotions that allows them to connect with a lost or confused teenager and build the trust that can enable meaningful discussion. In a manufacturing setting, when new AI-powered equipment is introduced, a floor supervisor's ability to understand emotions plays a key role in dealing with their team's worries about job security.

Thinking Clearly in the Time of AI

But hold on, you might be wondering, "Isn't AI meant to handle our thinking?" In fact, it's the other way around. AI tools have made critical thinking more crucial than ever before. AI gives you a lot of information and analysis, but it's your thinking that makes this information useful.

A florist can predict demand for flowers in different seasons by using AI. AI could tell you to buy roses for Valentine's Day from last year's information, but you know from your own experience that a new romantic movie is making sunflowers the hot item this year. Imagine a librarian using AI to suggest books. The AI will point out popular titles based on what people read, but you can suggest something else that might appeal to a young reader's imagination.

The growing need for critical thinking is seen in every industry. A builder using AI for project planning must check if the suggested timelines take into account local weather patterns and supply chain issues. A physiotherapist using AI to look at how patients move should carefully check if the recommended exercises fit well with the patient's daily life and motivation.

Critical thinking helps professionals spot when AI suggestions may come from old or unhelpful structures. A marketing professional might see that AI suggestions based on past data don't consider recent cultural changes or local events that could impact how well a campaign does.

The Change in Communication

It might be surprising, but communication skills are even more important in a workplace that uses AI. You connect technology with what people need, turning data insights into practical use.

A plumber can use AI tools to find common problems or figure out job costs, but good communication is needed to help a homeowner understand why the quick fix suggested by AI may not be the best choice for the long run. A restaurant owner can use Google Gemini to look at customer feedback, but it's important to communicate well so the staff know how to improve their service based on what they learn.

This communication link is especially important when things don't go as expected. A beauty salon owner using AI for appointment scheduling needs to explain to clients why the AI might suggest certain time slots over others. A mechanic needs to explain why they're doing something differently than the AI diagnostic tool suggested, based on their years of experience with similar vehicles.

The ability to transform complex concepts into simple explanations is very important. This might include telling colleagues why AI recommendations should be changed, helping customers see how AI tools improve personalised service instead of replacing it, or showing team members how to better use new AI features in their work.

The Growing Importance of Making Ethical Choices

As AI systems make more choices, human ethical judgement is becoming more important. Think about these important things that only people can really assess:

- How choices impact real people in your community

- Whether suggestions match your personal and work values

- If something is the right thing to do, not just the easy thing to do

An estate agent can use AI to improve property listings and forecast market trends, but it requires careful thought to determine how to manage information that could either increase profits or better meet a family's long-term needs. A small business owner can use AI to find ways to save money, but they should consider how this affects their support for local suppliers and the quality of their products.

These ethical choices happen in daily life. A recruitment consultant using AI for candidate screening should make sure that the tool does not unintentionally favour specific groups of people over others. A financial advisor using AI to recommend investments needs to balance possible profits with their client's personal values and comfort level with risk.

Small businesses encounter moral challenges when using AI. A supermarket that uses AI to manage its inventory might focus on being efficient, which could negatively affect local suppliers. A pharmacy using AI for stock predictions might prioritise profit instead of the needs of the community.

The New Human Edge

A new type of professional is on the rise—one who mixes their current skills with an understanding of AI. If you're a chef using AI to think of new recipes to complement your cooking style or maybe a carpenter working with AI design tools to complement your skills, your strength is not competing with AI but working with it.

Looking Ahead

In the next section, we will look at how to connect your current skills to specific AI opportunities. But keep this in mind: the skills that define us as humans—like judgement, empathy, critical thinking, communication, and ethical reasoning—are not going away. They are turning into your most valuable work resources.

Consider this: In a world where AI can create a thousand choices in just seconds, being able to pick the right one is very valuable.

In the next section, we will explore how to connect these human skills with specific AI opportunities in your area. Prepare to view your current skills from a fresh perspective.

***

Connecting Your Skills to AI Opportunities

Think about this: Every day, people in many jobs are finding that their current skills are more valuable than they thought in the age of AI. The florist who naturally understands how to mix colours and textures is suited to check AI-generated design ideas. A mechanic who can identify issues just by listening to an engine has important skills for monitoring AI systems.

Discovering the Talents You Already Have

Look at the skills that you use daily without even noticing. A hairstylist does more than cut hair. They understand body language, take very vague descriptions, turn them into clear actionable steps, and build trust with their skills and communication. The skills required for successful AI implementation are the same ones listed here.

Many professionals are already good at:

- Understanding small signals and body movements

- Turning unclear thoughts into clear steps

- Creating trust by showing knowledge

- Making decisions based on what you have learnt

- Changing ways of doing things based on quick feedback

These skills can be used directly when working with AI tools.

Your Everyday Skills Viewed Through AI

The skills you think are simple could be just what organisations need for successful AI integration. Think about how regular job skills can turn into useful abilities in the age of AI:

When you change how you communicate with different people, you show the ability to help team members understand and use AI tools. Being able to identify when something seems off or not right is important when checking AI results. That feeling for when to look closer or delve a little deeper? Knowing when to trust AI suggestions and when to take an even closer look is very important.

The Great Skill Translation

This is where things become interesting. Let's explore how common skills can turn into useful tools in the age of AI:

If you are skilled at... → You're likely really good at...

- Understanding people → Identifying when AI requires human intervention

- Dealing with complaints → Handling issues with AI implementation

- Making things easy to understand → Bringing AI skills to teams

- Finding patterns → Recognising AI opportunities

- Making decisions → Understanding when to rely on AI results

The best AI projects usually happen when teams combine their usual skills with AI technology. It's not about taking away human skills—it's about making them better with AI help.

Changing Skills

Moving to AI-enhanced roles doesn't mean you have to change who you are. It's about using your current skills in different ways. Think about these natural changes:

Skills in customer service naturally lead to an ability to implement AI because both need the following:

- Getting to know what users find frustrating

- Looking for useful answers

- Explaining complicated ideas in a simple way

- Creating trust with reliable support

Experience in managing people fits well with supervising AI because the basic skills are similar:

- Checking how well things are working

- Finding ways to do things better

- Making sure the results are good

- Giving helpful advice

Many people in different jobs easily move into AI positions. The ability to change a recipe, from a chef's perspective, based on the available ingredients might be the same as changing an AI-generated meal plan in cooking. Attention to detail and quality of carpentry are important when considering an AI-designed piece. A gardener's understanding of seasonal changes can help them verify that the AI-recommended maintenance schedule is correct.

Views from the Industry

There is a chance to bring together human skills and AI abilities in many areas. Think about how various professionals can help with AI implementation:

In retail, the knowledge that front-line workers have about customer behaviour can be very helpful in creating and using AI-powered customer service tools. Healthcare professionals' careful attention and ability to observe patients can help make sure AI tools are used correctly in clinical settings. Teachers' experience in spotting learning patterns can help create better AI-supported teaching methods.

This mix of human skill and AI ability appears in surprising areas. A painter knows how light changes colour, which helps them use AI tools to suggest colour schemes. A personal trainer understands what motivates each person, allowing them to adjust workout plans created by AI in a helpful way. A chef knows the local flavours, which helps them change AI-recommended menu items to fit their local community's likes and dislikes

It's becoming clear that successful AI use probably needs both technical skills and practical work experience. The best way is to mix AI skills with a clear understanding of what people need and how they act in different situations.

More Than Just Technical Skills

People are often surprised by the most desired features in AI implementation. Organisations aren't just looking for technical skills; they need professionals who can:

- Use their judgement to decide when human understanding is more important than AI suggestions.

- Turn technical abilities into useful business solutions

- Find suitable situations for using AI.

- Identify possible ethical issues before they turn into problems.

- Connect what AI can do with what people need

- Make sure AI solutions match the values and culture of the organisation.

These are not skills you pick up in a technical class; they come from actual work experience.

These skills are helpful in everyday life. A veterinary nurse may have to choose between following AI-recommended treatment plans and relying on their own experience in animal behaviour. A hotel manager might have to balance AI-driven pricing with local events while still maintaining good relationships with regular customers. A construction supervisor may need to adjust AI-created project timelines based on what they know about their team's skills and the conditions at a site.

How to Use Professional Judgement in Real Life

Using professional judgement is very important when applying AI suggestions to real-life situations. Think about how this operates in various situations:

From a hospitality perspective, restaurant managers know that AI-recommended staffing levels may need to be changed due to historical data for factors such as weather, local events or even the preferences of regular customers

Electricians know when AI-recommended wiring solutions need to be replaced due to the age of the building. It could also be because of local regulations or the condition of the place.

A specialist boutique owner understands when to change AI inventory suggestions by keeping an eye on local fashion trends and what customers like.

Looking Forward

As we prepare for Chapter 3, remember this: You do not have to reinvent yourself for the AI era. What you've learnt over your career isn't losing value; it's becoming more important in ways you probably never thought of.

Think about this: When AI can easily process billions of pieces of information and make limitless choices, the skill to make thoughtful decisions based on years of experience and understanding is more important than ever.

What's Next

In Chapter 3, we will look at how to use these skills in AI-supported settings. You'll see that you're not beginning from nothing—you're building on a base of useful experience that's very relevant in today's AI world.

Keep in mind that the aim is not to compete with AI but to enhance it using the special human skills you have developed over the years. When you mix these skills with knowing what AI can do, you open up chances that neither people nor AI could reach by themselves.

Chapter Three

AI Reality Check

Understanding What's True and What's Not About AI

When people hear about AI today, they think of tools like ChatGPT, Microsoft Copilot, Claude, or Google Gemini. Such tools are referred to as generative AI and can produce new content such as writing, ideas, and analysis based on what they have learnt. It helps to know what these tools are and the things they can do without getting technical.

The Current State of AI

AI tools are becoming more common in workplaces across different industries. Just like email changed how we communicate at work and spreadsheets changed how we manage data, AI tools are changing how we do a variety of our jobs. Knowing these tools helps you adjust to the changing workplace environment easily.

Understanding AI Tools of Today

Imagine generative AI as a helpful assistant that knows a lot and can assist with various tasks. These AI tools can create text, offer ideas, assist with analysis, and manage different tasks. They learn a lot from loads of information and can answer your questions in a range of helpful ways.

Today, these tools help with different work needs. Every day, they are being used more frequently by professionals to help them with things such as creating business documents and analysing data trends. They aren't magical or flawless, but they can be useful if used carefully.

What These Tools Can Do and What They Can't Complete

AI tools can assist with everyday tasks such as writing emails, making reports, or examining information. They can do lots of different tasks:

- Understanding Questions: When you ask them something, they usually get what you mean and can give helpful answers. AI tools can write answers to common questions or explain things that are hard to understand.

- Processing Information: These tools can take large amounts of information and help you understand it. Shortening long documents, highlighting important points, or finding specific details across a large amount of data can all be done.

- Offering Ideas: They can provide various ways or answers to the issues you bring up. This ability is useful for coming up with ideas, solving problems, and looking at challenges in a new way.

- Help with Projects: They can help with project planning, simplifying tasks, and giving ideas for tackling various parts of a project.

But these tools also have key limitations that professionals should be aware of:

1.They Need Human Supervision

They can make content and offer ideas, but they need people to review what they deliver to be sure it's correct and suitable. This check is important for keeping professional standards and making sure the work is of good quality.

2. They Work with What They Know

They can only use the information they have been trained on—they can't get current information unless they are specifically designed for that, like Google Gemini. This means they may not have the most current information about your industry or particular situation.

3. They Don't Really Understand

Even though they are very smart, they don't really understand what people understand. They work by looking for patterns or trends in the data, and they sometimes miss obvious context or details that a human being would easily understand.

Common Myths

A few common misunderstandings about today's AI tools need to be cleared up:

"AI Tools Will Replace People"

AI tools are actually most effective when they help people improve their work instead of necessarily taking over. Just like a calculator, it's a useful tool that makes certain tasks easier, but it also requires human judgement. Skill, imagination, and good judgement are still very important.

"AI Tools Have All the Answers"

These tools can occasionally get things wrong or give wrong information. They need people to check and oversee what they deliver. Using good judgement is important when checking and confirming their results.

"AI Tools Are Hard to Use."

A lot of AI tools are designed to be easy to use. If you know how to use email or a search engine, you can easily learn how to use AI tools to be successful. Start with simple tasks and gradually increase how you use them.

How to Use AI Tools Effectively

Working with AI tools requires knowing how they fit into what you do. They work best when used to:

1.Improve Your Work

Use them to make what you do better, not to completely alter how you work. This could involve creating a first version of content that you improve later or receiving ideas that you check using your experience.

2. Save Time

Allow them to assist with tasks that take a lot of time, so you can concentrate on work that requires your judgement and skills. This might involve regular paperwork, starting research, or simple analysis.

3. Support Decision Making

Get information and suggestions from them, but make your own important decisions. They can add more views and information but should not take the place of critical thinking.

Exploring Real Benefits

AI tools can be very helpful when used correctly.

Simplifying Everyday Tasks: They can assist in writing everyday messages, arranging information, or coming up with basic ideas. This efficiency helps professionals concentrate on more important tasks.

Making Consistency Better: They can help keep quality steady in everyday tasks, making sure similar activities are done in the same way.

Help you make better choices: They can provide additional perspectives and information to help you make decisions or suggest new ideas or ways of thinking.

Working Together

Thinking about using AI in your work needs careful consideration.

Quality Guidelines: Clear quality control processes are required to maintain professional standards while using AI support.

Combining Work Processes: Getting the right mix of AI help and human effort makes work processes better.

Learning New Skills: Getting good at using AI tools while keeping your professional skills strong helps set you up for success in the future.

Moving Forward Confidently

What AI tools can and can't do will help you use them really well. Remember that these tools are there to assist you and not to take the place of your skill and judgement.

Consider this: How could knowing what these tools can really do help you use them better in your job?

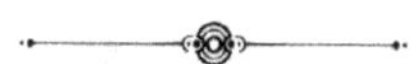

In the next section, we will look at some examples of how these tools can be used in real-life situations.

***

Practical Applications and Limitations

Now that we've looked at some common myths about AI, let's see what today's AI tools can actually do and what they can't do in real life. Knowing what they can really do helps us work better with them and understand what to expect.

What AI Tools Are Good At

You'll see that tools like ChatGPT, Microsoft Copilot, Claude, or Google Gemini are excellent at certain things. They handle text-based tasks such as writing emails, presenting a summary of a document, or suggesting solutions to problems and more, including image generation, etc.

Think about how spell-checkers have evolved over time. Early versions checked for spelling errors. Today's writing tools with AI can help you find better ways to say things, and they catch words when they are used incorrectly. This highlights both the progress AI makes and also the limits it has.

Understanding Current Limitations

For all they can do, AI tools still have limitations with regards to their capabilities. A calculator does maths well by calculating but does not have any idea of what the calculated numbers actually mean in everyday life. In the same way, AI tools need that human guidance.

They often have a hard time understanding the full context. They get it only from your inputs, but they would still need your inputs and wouldn't be able to run off with a prompt. Asking a colleague for a new business proposal or a business document comes with the understanding that the colleague knows your company situation, the market conditions, and any previous attempts at something similar. AI tools give ideas but rarely have a deeper understanding of your situation.

Emotions are also hard for them to understand. They recognise words that express emotion but not the subtle differences in emotions. This is useful for sensitive situations at work where understanding how people feel is important.

They are unable to make decisions in situations that are not clear. A skilled worker understands when it's okay to adjust normal rules due to unique situations. AI tools recognise patterns they've learnt, but they can't make complex decisions.

Where AI Tools Help Most

In workplaces, AI tools can improve our tasks in a few ways:

Work on Documents
These tools help with handling a lot of text and highlight important points. But you should check their work to ensure it meets your professional requirements and situation. A legal secretary might use AI to summarise case documents, but they need to make sure important details aren't missed.

Making Your First Draft
AI tools can help you get started with writing emails, reports, or presentations. You should modify what they create to fit your professional requirements and style.

Spotting Patterns
AI tools can find patterns in information that could be interesting to further investigate. Your knowledge helps figure out if these patterns are important and

what actions to take with regards to them. A café owner might use AI to look at sales patterns, but they also need their local knowledge to know if these patterns are ongoing patterns or just short-term changes.

Analysing Data

AI tools are great at handling a lot of information fast. But figuring out what the analysis means for your situation requires expert opinion. A property manager can use AI to look at maintenance records, but they still use their experience to decide which problems should be attended to immediately.

Key Points to Keep in Mind

Knowing what AI tools can't do helps manage expectations:

- They rely on others to make decisions. They can offer suggestions based on what they've observed, but they can't determine what's suitable in complicated situations.

- They don't see how things affect the real world. They handle information but don't understand how their suggestions could impact actual real-world scenarios.

- They can collect ideas that already exist but not think of new ones. They can suggest interesting combinations of things that are already there, but they can't come up with new ideas like humans.

Using AI Tools to Your Advantage

Knowing these strengths and weaknesses helps us use AI tools better. For instance, a retail manager may use AI to identify sales trends, but they will need to rely on their understanding of the local market to fully understand the impact of these trends.

An HR professional can use AI to create policy documents, but they must make sure these documents align with the company's culture and values.

A marketing expert can use AI to look at customer feedback, but they will need their skills to determine what changes to implement based on said feedback.

Working Together with AI

Success comes from understanding what AI can and cannot do. It's about understanding how AI tools can make your work better and knowing when your own judgement is most important.

This partnership works best when you:

- Use AI to get started with ideas or drafts

- Use your knowledge to look at the suggestions

- Change suggestions based on practical experience

- Keep an eye on quality at every step

As AI tools get better, they will assist with more tasks. However, they will always require human guidance to make sure their work is up to professional standards and is practical in real life.

Looking Forward

Knowing what AI tools can and can't do helps you use them better. Think about the usual tasks you do at work. Which tasks could AI tools assist with? In what situations would your professional judgement still be important?

In Chapter 4, we will explore some AI tools and how to begin using them, thinking about what they can do and what they can't.

Part 2: Essential Skills and Tools

Chapter Four

Getting Started with AI Tools

Key AI Tools for Non-Technical Professionals

In the previous chapters, we looked at how to turn AI worries into opportunities while appreciating the worth of your job skills. Now let's look at the tools that can help you put these ideas into action. If you're unsure about how to start working with AI tools, you're not the only one—many professionals feel this way when starting their AI journey.

Starting Your AI Journey

This chapter serves as your starting point for the tools that can improve the skills we talked about before. You don't have to be a technical expert to make good use of these tools. They are made to fit with the skills you already possess.

The World of AI Tools

Imagine this situation: You're standing in the middle of a kitchen that has every-thing you need. There are lots of utensils, and each one is made for a particular job. Some seem familiar, while others are very different. Many professionals feel this way when they first start using AI tools. Let's make this area easier to get around.

Learning About Different AI Tools

When professionals first see AI tools, they often wonder, "Which one is best for me?" It all depends on what you want to accomplish. Some tools are simpler to learn but may have fewer features, while others require more time to master but provide more options. We'll start looking at how these tools stack up against each other.

Learning About Tool Types

Think about AI tools in terms of two main aspects: how simple they are to use and the potential impact they can have. Some tools are easy to learn but may only be useful in a few situations, while others take more time to learn but can do a lot more things.

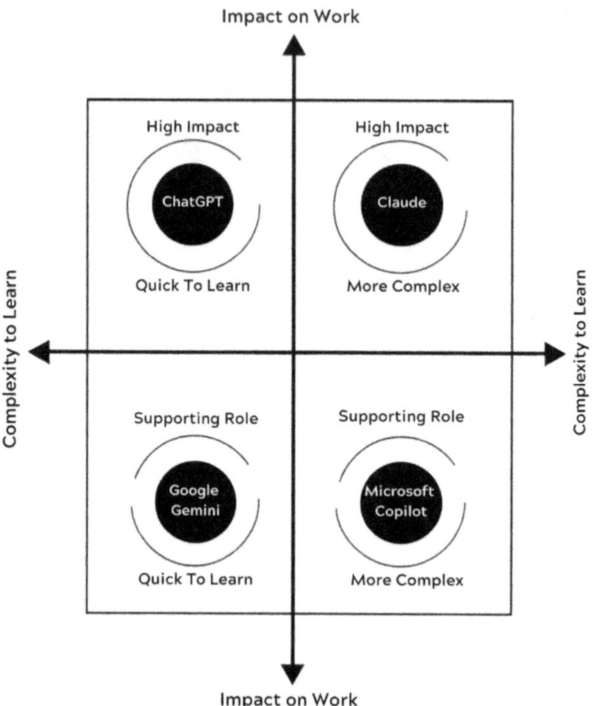

Learning About Important AI Tools

Before we look at specific tools, it's important to remember that AI as a whole is evolving quickly, with new tools coming out all the time and updates to existing tools. This section looks at a few common tools that many professionals use, but it is just a small part of what is out there. Here are some popular tools you might think about adding to your work toolkit:

ChatGPT

This tool works well as a helper for daily work tasks. It works well for writing emails, outlines of documents, and quick answers to questions. Many people start using ChatGPT because it has a simple interface and can be used for simple work tasks.

Claude

This tool is particularly good at detailed analysis. Claude is useful for long projects and detailed research tasks that require clear answers that meet specific needs.

Google Gemini

Very useful when searching for information. It helps in researching and reviewing facts, and ultimately, it can be a useful tool for keeping track of information in your field.

These tools are just examples as you start out on your AI journey. You will likely find other options that are better suited to your needs, and as AI evolves, new tools will become available. Always keep an eye out and keep testing them to see which fit best.

Figuring Out Which Tool Work Best

This table shows how these tools compare in different areas:

Tool Aspect	ChatGPT	Claude	Google Gemini
Best AI	Quick help with everyday tasks	Detailed analysis and longer projects	Finding current information
How Easy to Learn	Very easy	Takes some practice	Fairly easy
Quality of Work	Good for most needs	Very detailed	Good with current topics
Things to Watch For	Check facts carefully	Can be very detailed	Check information

Using These Tools Every Day

These tools can assist you during your workday:

In the morning:
Use them to plan your day, like writing emails. They can help you start your day on the front foot and even arrange to-do actions from the previous day

During main work hours:
They can assist you with writing documents, researching topics, and solving problems. Think of them as helpers that can simplify your tasks.

End of day:
Use them to sum up what you've done for the day, get ready for tomorrow, and sort your notes out.

Getting Started: Your First Steps

Do you remember when you learnt how to drive? You didn't start off on the motorway. Start with easy applications:

Start with Easy Tasks: Set your sights on straightforward activities that you do often, such as writing regular emails, making plans, or outlining simple documents.

Work on simple projects that have less pressure on them. Start with internal documents or personal projects that aren't as important or critical.

Build Confidence Slowly: Just like with any new skill, the more you practice and try things out, the better you'll get.

Tips for Success

Start with one tool and get really good using it before adding more—give ChatGPT a try.

Always double-check important information by looking at different sources.

Track effective prompts and methods you use

Looking Ahead

As you become more familiar with these tools, you'll discover more ways they can assist you in your work. Next, we'll look at how to create your own set of AI tools that suit your specific needs.

Think about this: What simple task could you get started with one of these tools?

In the next section, we will look at how to use these tools together so that they work effectively for you.

***

Building Your AI Toolkit

Look at the different tools that you use in your job right now. You likely picked them to help you work more efficiently, unless they were already selected for you, but there may be some you have introduced to make your life a little easier. Creating your AI toolkit is similar—you should pick AI tools that match your needs and your preferred way of working.

Starting Your AI Journey

Now that you are familiar with some AI tools from the previous section, let's explore how to select and mix the right ones for your tasks. There's no need to use all the AI tools out there, but there's also no limit if you want to—just pick the ones that will be the most useful for you.

Picking Tools That Work for You

Before you add any new AI tools to your daily tasks, take a minute and think about what you do every day. What are the things that take up most of your time? Which ones do you seem to constantly repeat? These are usually the best places for you to start looking at AI assistance.

For example, if you send a lot of emails, you may want to look for tools that assist with writing. If you look at a lot of information, you may want tools that help review, organise, and summarise the information.

How Different Tools Work Together

Here is a table with a few simple tips for matching tools with some common work-related needs:

What You Need to Do	Main Tool to Use	Helper Tool	How to Use Them
Writing (emails, reports)	ChatGPT	Claude	Use ChatGPT for first drafts, Claude to make them better
Finding Information	Google Gemini	ChatGPT	Use Google Gemini to find current info, and ChatGPT to explain it clearly
Deep Analysis	Claude	Microsoft Copilot	Use Claude for detailed work and Microsoft Copilot for specific tasks
Creating Documents	Microsoft Copilot	ChatGPT	Use Microsoft Copilot within Microsoft tools, ChatGPT for extra help

Getting Tools to Work Together

Using different AI tools together will give you the best results. This is how it works:

When you need to write something important, you can start with ChatGPT to help you organise your main ideas. You can use Claude to make your writing clearer and more detailed. It's like having two helpers instead of just one.

Sometimes, you may have to take things one step at a time. You could use Google Gemini to find new information, then use ChatGPT to sort it out, summarise, and finally use Claude to add more detail. Every tool has its own specific use.

Building Your Skills

Start off with one tool and get used to it before you move on to others. This will help you gain confidence and grow your skills step by step. Today, a lot of people get success by starting with ChatGPT for basic tasks and then moving on to more specific tools as their needs increase. This doesn't mean you should limit yourself to just ChatGPT as a starting point. It's more of a suggestion, but you may want to start with Google Gemini or any others, but the simplicity of ChatGPT makes it a good starting point.

Think about improving your skills step by step:

Starting Phase
Pick one AI tool that helps you the most. For example, if you often write emails and reports, focus on learning how ChatGPT can help you with those tasks. Take time to learn how to achieve the best outcomes by following clear steps and making sure that you are ALWAYS reviewing what's produced.

Middle Phase
After you start growing in confidence and feel good with your first tool, think about adding another one that works well with your needs. If you started

out with ChatGPT for writing, you could try Claude for deeper analysis or Microsoft Copilot for organising your documents.

Advanced Phase

As you become more confident, look into how different tools can work together to boost your productivity. This might include creating processes that use different tools one after the other, with each tool focusing on what it does best.

Choosing the Right Tools

When you're thinking about adding a new AI tool for your job, think about this:

- Will this tool help with tasks that I do regularly? Only include tools that will help you with your everyday tasks.

- Will it work well with my other tools? The best tools integrate smoothly with regards to how you already work.

- How much time will it take to learn? Make sure that the time you spend learning will be useful for the support you will get in return.

Keeping Your Tools Working Well

Your AI tools, like any other work tool, need your attention. Make sure to always check if each tool is really making your work easier. Sometimes a tool that looked helpful at first may not be as useful as time goes. Keep an eye out for updates to your tools. AI tools frequently receive updates that can improve your work processes.

Creating Positive Habits

Using AI tools to build good habits helps keep your work quality and efficiency consistent. Think about setting up these habits:

Quality Control Step

Find a way to make sure the AI-generated information is correct This could mean checking facts, confirming calculations, and making sure the tone of voice and style fit your professional standards.

Documentation

Keep clear notes of what works well and the prompts that are effective. This documentation becomes more valuable as you use more tools and take on more complex tasks.

Regular Review

Plan regular checks on how you use your AI tools:

- Check which tools are giving the most value

- Find places where processes can be improved

- Have a think if new tools could improve how you work

- Check if the tools you have are still working for you and meeting your needs

Improving Your Skills

Growing professionally with AI tools is about more than just learning new features. It involves knowing how these tools can improve your skills and career opportunities.

Skill Development

Think about how AI tools could assist you:

- Work on bigger projects

- Improve the quality of work

- Manage more tasks

- Build new skills for your career

Planning for the Future

Imagine how AI could change your job. Keep up to date with updates that could boost your effectiveness, but pay attention to changes that provide real benefits for what you do.

Moving Forward

As we move into Chapter 5, think about how you can start using these tools in your own work. Remember, the objective isn't to use as many tools as possible, but to find the ones that make your work easier and more efficient—work smarter, not harder.

Think about this: What is one thing you do on a daily basis that could be made easier with the right AI tool?

In Chapter 5, we'll look at how to use these tools effectively and how you can stay away from common mistakes that beginners often make with AI.

Chapter Five

The AI Learning Curve

Effective Learning Strategies

After looking at different AI tools, you may be wondering about how to use them successfully. Just like getting used to a new mobile phone (and hopefully avoiding those accidental photo deletions), there's a way to handle this learning process effectively.

Knowing Where You Begin

Our journey into AI tools builds on the knowledge we talked about in previous chapters. Think about how you learnt to do your current job—you likely began with the basics and improved as you went along. Learning AI tools is similar—with less pressure to look busy during training sessions.

Learning AI Made Easy

We naturally learn to use AI tools better over time. Imagine it as a path where every step adds to the previous one:

```
Foundation → Development → Integration → Mastery
     ↑                                         ↓
     ← ← ← ← ← Continuous Learning ← ← ← ←
```

Let's break down what happens at each stage of this journey:

Stage	What You'll Do	What You'll Gain
Foundation	Learn the basics of using AI tools	Confidence with everyday tasks
Development	Try different ways to use the tools	Knowledge of which tool works best when
Integration	Make AI tools part of your daily work	More efficient ways of working
Mastery	Explore advanced features	Better results with less effort

Finding Your Learning Style

People learn to use AI tools in lots of different ways. Some people prefer to dive in and learn by experimenting, just like checking the temperature of a swimming pool. Some people like to learn gradually, focusing on one feature at a time.

Both options can be effective. Think about how you typically learn new tools for your job—that same approach could work for learning AI tools as well.

Learning in Real Life

Learning AI tools is easier when you see how they can help you in your everyday job.

A retail manager could start by using AI to write simple replies to customers. Then, they could use AI to understand what customers are saying about their shop. Finally, they could use AI to create better plans for customer service.

A tradesperson could start by using AI to calculate the number of materials they need. Then, they could use AI to write detailed quotes for customers. Finally, they could use AI to project plan entire projects.

A healthcare administrator could start by using AI to schedule appointments. Then, they could use AI to write messages to patients. Finally, they could use AI to make their clinic run more smoothly.

Improving Your Abilities

You can learn to use AI tools just like you learnt your current job skills, one step at a time. Start with tasks where mistakes won't matter so much; this helps you learn at your own pace and steadily build confidence.

Getting Started: Start with easy tasks that you already do regularly. This allows you to see how AI tools could help with tasks you already know.

Improving Your Abilities: Once you get comfortable, try some tasks that are a bit more challenging. Write down what works well; it will be useful later.

Common Challenges You Might Face

Learning to use AI tools can be tough. There are so many to choose from, it's easy to feel lost. Start with just one tool that can help you with tasks you do often.

Finding time to learn AI can be hard too, especially when you're busy with work. Try setting aside just 15 minutes each day to experiment with AI tools. A little bit of practice goes a long way.

Making It Work for You

Here are a few approaches that could be useful:

Regular Practice: Choose a certain time each day or week to learn. Even just 15 minutes can help you get better over time.

Keep Track of What Is Working: Note down helpful methods as you find them. This helps you make your own guide for using AI tools well.

Moving Forward with Confidence

Remember, everyone starts somewhere, even with new tools like AI. You already know a lot about your job, and that knowledge you have will help you learn how AI can make your work easier.

Don't worry about learning everything at once. Focus on small steps and steady progress.

Looking Ahead

In the next section, we'll look at common challenges when it comes to learning AI tools and, more importantly, how to try to avoid them. Learning something new should make your job simpler, not more difficult.

In the next section, we will look at these common mistakes and share some straightforward ways to avoid them.

***

Common Mistakes and How to Avoid Them

Now that we've looked at ways to learn AI tools, let's go through some common challenges that people come across—and, more importantly, how to deal with them. Think of this as a friendly reminder about the challenges you might face, like a colleague giving you tips about a similar project they've already completed

Figuring Out Where People Usually Have Trouble

When learning to use AI tools, most of us face similar challenges. Learning to drive can be a bit stressful at times (like when you have to parallel park), and using AI tools also has some challenging parts. Let's look at some of the most common ones and how to manage them as best as possible.

The "Too Much, Too Soon" Problem

One of the biggest mistakes is to try to learn everything at once. It's like trying to read a whole cookbook at once—you might know what's in it, but it won't help you cook any better.

Here's a simpler way to do it:

Instead of...	Try This
Learning three AI tools at once	Get good at one tool that you use a lot
Trying advanced features straight away	Start with basic features you'll use often
Completely changing your work routine	Slowly add AI into what you already do

The Accuracy Assumption

Some people start trusting AI tools straight away, while others are more cautious about putting their trust in them. Think of AI as a smart apprentice who can assist you but needs some guidance. Here's what to look out for:

When to Check Again:

- Important information and figures

- Client-facing communications

- Industry-specific information

- Anything that might impact business decisions

When to Trust the Process:

- First drafts and outlines

- General ideas and recommendations

- Basic research starting points

- Creative brainstorming

The Myth of the "Perfect Output"

Many people think AI tools should give perfect results right from the start. Similar to thinking you can speak fluent French after just one lesson. Instead, think of what AI generates as an initial draft that needs your expertise to correct.

Let's think about how this works in real life. A legal secretary can use AI to write legal documents. But they'll still need to check the documents to make sure they're correct and meet the client's needs. A marketing team could use AI to write blog posts, but they'll still need to make sure the posts sound like their brand and help them sell products. An estate agent could use AI to write descriptions of houses, but they'll still need to add information about the local area and what makes each house special.

Finding the Right Balance

Here's how to balance using AI tools while keeping your professional judgement:

Area	Watch Out For	Better Approach
Time Management	Spending too long perfecting prompts	Set a time limit for each task
Quality Control	Accepting AI-generated outputs without reviewing them	Treat AI as a first draft helper
Learning Pace	Rushing to the advanced features	Master the basics before moving forward
Work Integration	Forcing AI into every task	Use AI only where it helps

Learning From Experience

When we learn a new tool, we usually get better by figuring out what works and what doesn't. With AI tools, keeping track of this makes a big difference.

Every day, write down the basic things that happen in your job:

- What tasks worked well with AI assistance

- Where you needed to make lots of changes

- What you might try differently next time

For example, you might find that AI tools are great for writing simple social media posts, but you may need to add your own personal touch to more important posts. Or you might find out that certain ways of asking for what you want get better results than others.

Setting Realistic Expectations

As with any new work skill, getting good at using AI tools takes time. Realistic expectations help with the learning process.

Remember:

- You don't need to be perfect right away

- It's fine to start with simple tasks

- Everyone has to learn as they go

- Getting help from colleagues is normal

Avoiding Common Communication Mistakes

When using AI tools for communication, be careful not to make common mistakes. AI might write perfect emails, but they might not sound like you. Take the time to change the tone of voice to match your style. Remember, AI doesn't know your company or your customers. Make sure to add relevant information to any AI-generated content, such as specific details about your company's products or services or the unique needs of your customers.

Being Smart About Company Information

Think about your company's rules about using AI tools for work tasks before using them. Just as you wouldn't share private work documents on social media, you should be careful about what company information you share with AI tools.

Why is this important? Well, when you type information into AI tools such as ChatGPT, that information may be saved and used later. It's like writing something on a public whiteboard—others might see it after you're done.

Some simple tips to stay safe:

- Check if your company has rules about using AI tools

- Think twice before sharing specific company details

- Use general examples instead of real company data

- When in doubt, ask your manager

Don't worry—we'll take a closer look at this in Chapter 8, where we'll explore how to use AI tools responsibly at work. For now, just remember to think carefully about the company information you share with AI tools.

Keeping on the Right Path

Here's an easy way to see if you're using AI tools well:

Ask yourself:

- Is this making my work easier or just different?

- Am I taking longer to correct AI results than it would take to do the job myself?

- Does the end result still show my professional judgement?

If any answers worry you, it could be a good idea to change how you're doing things.

Making Changes as You Progress

Remember that learning curve we talked about earlier? Here's a practical way to handle the bumps:

Have a section for quick notes:

- What worked well today?

- What needed lots of changes?

- What might work better next time?

This should help you learn from your mistakes and successes.

Creating Better Habits

As you start using AI tools, try to develop a few good habits.

First, take a few minutes each week to think about what's working and what isn't. This will help you avoid bad habits and improve your work processes.

Second, focus on learning one new thing about your AI tool each week. It's like learning a new recipe. Start with one new thing at a time, and soon you'll be a master chef.

Being Smart About Company Information

Before using AI tools for work tasks, there's something important to think about: your company's rules about using them. Just like you wouldn't share sensitive work documents on social media, you need to be careful about what company information you share with AI tools.

If you type something into AI tools like ChatGPT, that information might be saved and used later on. Anyone could read what you wrote even after you have finished.

Here are a few easy ways to keep safe:

- Check if your company has rules about using AI tools

- Think twice before sharing specific company details

- Use general examples instead of real company data

- When in doubt, ask your manager

With regards to using AI tools responsibly at work, we'll take a closer look at this in Chapter 8. For now, just remember to think carefully about the company information you share with AI tools.

Looking Ahead

Remember, every professional who's good at using AI tools started exactly where you are. The goal isn't to be perfect; it's to be better today than you were yesterday.

Think about this: Which of these potential concerns is most related to your job? Knowing this helps you stay alert to it as you continue your AI journey.

In Chapter 6, we will look at how to talk about AI clearly with your coworkers and teams, making sure everyone benefits from these tools.

Part 3: Making AI Work for You

Chapter Six

Working with AI in Teams

Effective Communication About AI

You should slowly be getting comfortable with AI tools and how they can help you work by now. But what if you have to work on projects with others? A few of your colleagues might be looking forward to AI, while others may be unsure or worried.

Starting the Conversation

Think about how you'd explain a new mobile phone feature to a friend. You wouldn't start with technical details. You'd probably focus on how it makes their life easier. The same approach works when talking about AI tools with your colleagues.

**Setting the Right Context

Before getting into the details, it's important to link AI to what your team aims to achieve together and what matters to you all. What are the objectives? Start by identifying the strengths your team already has. For example, if your team values customer service, talk about how AI tools can help keep those high standards while managing more customer enquiries. If quality has always been your focus, explain how AI can help maintain that quality even when the workload increases.

Kick off the conversation around improving your team's skills instead of replacing them. When team members see that AI helps them achieve their professional goals instead of being a threat to their jobs, they are more likely to use these new tools positively.

Getting to Know Different Perspectives

You might find your teammates fall into different groups when it comes to AI:

Approach to AI	What You Might Hear	How to Help
Curious but Cautious	"I'm interested but don't know where to start."	Share simple, practical examples from your own experience
Very Resistant	"I'd rather do things the way I know."	Show small improvements in everyday tasks
Over-Enthusiastic	"Let's use AI for everything!"	Help focus on practical, valuable uses
Already Using It	"Have you tried this feature?"	Exchange tips and learn from each other

Making It Relevant

When talking about AI with colleagues, focus on actual work scenarios that they face. A marketing team may find it helpful to know that AI can assist in creating social media posts while keeping the brand's voice consistent. Customer service representatives may find it useful to know how AI can recommend smart replies based on past conversations, helping them keep on top of things during busy periods.

Give concrete examples from your own experience: "Remember that monthly report that takes forever to format?" I can show you how I cut that down to 20 minutes." Or "You know those client emails you spend a lot of time writing?" Here's how AI tools can help with the first draft so you can speed up the process.

For creative teams, highlight how AI can take care of simple tasks like basic image editing or formatting, allowing more time for the creative work that truly requires their skills. Office teams might find it helpful to learn how AI can assist in organising meeting notes or creating presentation outlines, allowing them to concentrate on improving their message and delivery.

Sharing Your Learning Journey

Being honest about your own experience helps other people connect. Talk about everything you did right and what you learnt the hard way. For example: "It took me a few tries to get used to AI, but I can't imagine doing my weekly summaries without it."

Being open about your challenges can make others feel more comfortable with their own learning journey.

Gaining Confidence by Practicing

Letting teams try out AI in a safe way is important for them to accept the technology. Think about setting up casual "AI coffee breaks" where colleagues can talk about what they've learnt or found out and ask questions in a relaxed atmosphere with no pressure. These sessions are most effective when they are optional and concentrate on practical aspects instead of theory.

People teach and learn from each other. Whenever you can, pair up experienced AI users with those who are just starting out. This creates a natural way for people to mentor each other and helps everyone learn. Celebrating even the smallest of wins and achievements can help the team be more open to using AI.

Managing Team Dynamics

Knowing how team members relate to each other is important for successfully implementing AI. Every team has informal influencers—colleagues whose views matter more. Finding these team members and showing them how AI tools can help can really boost the team's use of these tools.

Different team members learn in different ways. Some people like to sit and read instructions; others prefer the practical approach and learn better by doing things themselves. Some people like watching others or videos of how all things are done. If you make sure there are different ways to learn about AI tools, it helps everyone get involved in a way that suits them.

Collaborating with AI Tools

When using AI tools in team projects, try to remember these points:

Clear Communication:
- Let others know when you're using AI tools.

- Tell me how you are checking the results.

- Share any helpful prompts you've found.

Team Approach:
- Accept that some team members may choose to use methods that don't involve AI.

- Concentrate on the outcomes instead of the tools used.

- Share improvements in a way that helps everyone.

Dealing with Everyday Issues

Here are some common situations you may come across:

When Someone is Worried About Their Job:

- Look at how AI helps with boring tasks.

- Highlight how it allows for more time to focus on more important tasks.

- Share examples of how AI improves skills instead of replacing them.

When There is Pushback for Change:

- Start with small, low-risk things.

- Show people rather than constantly telling them.

- Let results speak for themselves.

Making It Work for Everyone

Remember that good teamwork isn't about everyone using the same tools; it's about working well together. Here are a few tips:

- Keep track of what works best for different tasks.

- Be open to using both AI and non-AI methods.

- Focus on what helps the team succeed.

Looking Ahead

As you keep using AI tools, you'll find more ways to help your team make the most of them. It's important to make sure that everyone feels comfortable with how quickly things are changing.

Think about this: What's the one task your team does regularly that could be easier with AI tools?

In the next section, we will look at ways of creating effective team practices using AI tools, making sure everyone can take part and gain from them.

***

Building Teamwork in AI

Now that we've looked at how to talk about AI with your colleagues, let's look at some simple ways to effectively use AI tools in your team. Imagine bringing in a new tool for your job—it's not only about having it but also about using it in a way that helps everyone.

Making a Common Plan

Teams succeed when everyone knows how things work. Here's an easy way to think about how to use AI tools together:

```
Individual Skills → Team Sharing → Best Practices → Regular Updates
            ↑                                                    ↓
        ← ← ← ← ← ← Learning & Improving ← ← ← ← ← ←
```

How to Use AI for Your Team

Different teams need different approaches. Here's a practical guide to what works best:

Good Team Practices	Things to Watch Out For
Share useful prompts	Keeping helpful tips private
Document what works	Everyone doing their own thing
Learn from mistakes	Hiding problems
Regular check-ins	Working in isolation

Think about how your team handles new tools or processes right now. The same ideas that help you use any new tool at work also apply to AI. Having clear rules, talking openly, and supporting each other can turn challenges into success.

Setting Up Team Guidelines

Think about creating simple rules that help everyone collaborate smoothly. For instance:

Checking Quality

- Who checks AI-generated content?

- How do we keep our usual standards?

- What needs human supervision?

Sharing Information

- Where can we find helpful prompts?

- How can we share what is effective?

- When should we change our approach?

Making It Work Day-to-Day

Successful teams add AI discussions into their everyday work routines. In morning meetings, team members can talk about new findings or what worked well for them. "Yesterday, I found a great way to use AI for formatting client presentations. Let me explain how it works." Weekly reviews are chances to talk about which AI methods worked best, and monthly updates help teams look at the bigger picture and see how their work has improved.

Sharing and talking about AI tools regularly makes them a normal part of daily work and helps improve how they're used over time. It also provides a chance for team members to ask for help or talk about their successes.

Handling Different Skill Levels

Teams usually have people who are at different levels of comfort when it comes to using AI. Here's how to make it work:

The Experience Exchange

Team Member Type	How They Help	What They Need
AI Enthusiasts	Share new tips	Patience with others
Steady Learners	Ask good questions	Regular practice time
Careful Adopters	Spot potential issues	Extra support

Measuring Success Together

How do you know if your team is using AI effectively? Look for the following:

- Faster completion of normal tasks

- Fewer need for changes than normal

- Team members helping each other

- Extra time for creative tasks

Building a Culture of Continuous Improvement

Understanding the technology isn't enough to get the most from AI tools. It is also about developing a team that continuously learns and grows. Encourage team members to share their wins and difficulties. If someone finds a new method or faces a challenge, see it as a chance for the whole team to learn.

Regular feedback sessions help teams refine and improve their methods. Rather than waiting for formal reviews, set up casual opportunities for people to share ideas for improvements or for them to raise any concerns. This could be by setting aside some time in team meetings for discussions about AI or creating channels for sharing quick tips and findings.

Boosting Team Confidence

Keep these important points in mind:

- Celebrate the small wins

- Talk about improvements openly

- Help with different learning speeds

- Stay focused on team goals

Creating Helpful Resources

Think about setting up:

- A Team AI Toolkit

- Helpful prompts that work well

- Basic task templates

- Success stories

- Lessons learned along the way

Moving Forward Together

The best teams find ways to use AI tools that work for everyone. It's all about finding better ways to work together, not forcing change.

Think about this: How could your team start sharing AI knowledge in a better way?

In Chapter 7, we'll look at how to use AI in a responsible way, making sure your team's work stays secure and reliable.

Chapter Seven

Using AI Responsibly

Understanding Privacy and Security

When using AI tools at work, privacy and security are a priority. These tools can really improve our work, but we have to be careful about how we use them, especially when it comes to sensitive information. Let's look at some important parts of using AI tools safely in your job.

Understanding the Main Privacy and Security Risks

When using AI tools at work, there are three main risks to think about. Knowing this helps us make better decisions about what information to share and the best way to share it.

The first risk is that AI systems learn from what we give them. When you type information into an AI tool, you get a response, but that information doesn't disappear. The system may store and use this information to train itself to give better responses to any future questions. This means that if you go into specific details about your industry or company practices, that information may appear in responses from other users, including competitors.

The second risk is the chance of data breaches. Even though companies that offer AI tools have strong security measures in place, no digital system can be entirely secure. Banks put a lot of money into security, but they still tell customers to be careful with their information. We should be careful about what we share when it comes to AI tools.

The third risk is about third-party access. AI companies often hire external contractors who might access user data whilst performing system maintenance or improvement tasks. Even though these sorts of things have strict rules about privacy, it shows another way your information could be accessed by others.

How AI Tools Handle Information

When you use an AI tool, a few things happen with your information:

What Happens	What It Means	Why It Matters
Storage	Your input is saved	Your information stays even after you finish your session
Processing	AI reviews and analyses your input	The system is actively using your information
Learning	The system may use your information to improve	Your input could help shape future responses
Access	Your data may be seen by many	Your information might be viewed by others

Creating Useful Security Methods

Knowing these risks helps to create simple ways to use AI tools safely. Think of AI interactions as public conversations. Here are some ways to keep sensitive information safe while still enjoying the benefits of using AI:

When talking about how a business is doing, pay attention to trends and ranges instead of exact numbers. Instead of saying "Our Q3 sales were £2.5 million, up 15% from last year," try "Our quarterly sales grew by 10-20%."

When you need specific industry advice, ask general questions instead of sharing specific issues related to your company. Instead of saying, "At Johnson Manufacturing, we're having problems with supply chain delays," ask, "What can a manufacturing company do to improve supply chain efficiency?"

When you're working with client information, use general examples. Instead of saying "Need to draft a proposal for ABC Corporation's new IT system," try "Searching for proposal templates for enterprise IT projects."

Getting to Know Company Approaches

Different organisations use AI tools in different ways depending on how much risk they can tolerate and their security needs:

<u>The Standard Approach</u> allows employees to use public AI tools freely, but they should think carefully about the information they share. This works well for organisations that mainly handle public information or have solid security training programs.

<u>Restricted Access</u> means that the AI tool can only be used on certain approved platforms or special versions that have better security features. Organisations that deal with important client data or private information often select this method.

<u>Enterprise Solutions</u> provide AI tools designed to meet the security needs and internal guidelines of the organisation. This gives you the most control, but it needs a lot of money for setup and training.

Choosing Wisely

Think about these questions before sharing information with an AI tool:

Can this information help competitors? Think about whether the information you are about to share could give away details about how your company works, its plans, or how well it is doing.

Is this information really available to everyone? Think about whether the information you are sharing can be found in public sources or if it is something that should stay private.

Will senior management give their approval? Think about whether the leaders in your organisation would feel okay with this information being shared with an AI system.

Using Safe AI Practices

To use AI tools safely and effectively:

First, check your company's rules about using AI. Many organisations have clear rules about which tools can be used and how to manage different kinds of information. Knowing these limits allows you to work comfortably within safe guidelines.

When you need advice or examples, try not to share specific details. This allows you to use the AI tools and keep your sensitive information private. Try changing specific situations into general questions that keep private information safe.

If your organisation offers enterprise versions of AI tools, be aware of their extra security features. These can include things like data encryption, access controls, etc. that help keep sensitive information safe.

Building Lasting Security Habits

Create safe ways for using AI tools. Just as you have habits like locking your computer or keeping documents safe, rather than them being in public view, protect your information when using AI.

Think about making templates for usual AI conversations that easily remove sensitive information. This helps you work faster while keeping things secure. Checking your AI usage regularly can help you find ways to make it better.

Moving Forward Securely

As AI tools keep evolving, it's important to stay aware of security-related issues. Use these tools to keep sensitive information safe while also making the most of what they can do to improve your work.

Think about this: How can you change the way you use AI tools to keep sensitive information safe while still taking advantage of what they offer?

In the next section, we will look at how to make ethical choices when using AI tools, making sure we use them in a responsible and fair way.

***

Making Ethical AI Decisions

After understanding the privacy and security aspects of AI tools, let's look at how to use them responsibly in our jobs. Making ethical decisions about using AI isn't about complicated rules; it's about using good judgement in new situations.

Understanding Ethical Considerations

When we use AI tools at work, we need to think about how our choices affect others. For example, if we use AI to help write emails or messages to clients, we need to make sure that we are humanely genuine and have authentic relationships with the clients. When we use AI to look at data, we should think about any potential biases in the results. For example, if we use AI to help write emails or messages to clients, we need to make sure we maintain genuine and authentic relationships with our customers.

Important Areas for Making Ethical Decisions

Let's look at some important areas where ethics matter:

Transparency: When using AI tools for work that affects others, we need to be open about it. We don't need to say every time we use AI for simple tasks, but we should be truthful when it matters to others.

For example, instead of claiming that AI-generated content is completely your own work, a better way to position this could be: "I wrote this report with help from AI, and I've double checked it, so I'm happy with the content."

Fairness and Bias: AI tools can sometimes show biases in their answers. We need to keep an eye on this and make sure our work stays fair and balanced.

For example, when using AI for employee assessments, make sure you don't depend only on the evaluations that AI creates. When making content, make sure it's appropriate and inclusive for the audience you want to reach.

Making Smart Choices with AI Tools

When you're using AI tools, it's important to have and keep high ethical standards. The framework highlights important areas where you'll need to carefully decide how to use AI in the right way. This table gives guidance on how to keep professional integrity while using AI tools effectively. Think of these approaches as helpful tips to balance the benefits of AI tools with your work duties.

Area	Ethical Consideration	Appropriate Approach
Client Work	Maintaining high quality and being genuine	Use AI as a tool, but always use your own judgment
Team Collaboration	Being honest about AI usage	Let others know when AI tools really help with work
Decision Making	Always make sure a human is involved	Use AI to get ideas, but make your own decisions
Content Creation	Keep things original	Use AI to get started, then add your own unique skills and expertise

Guidelines for Using AI Responsibly

When using AI tools, keep these ideas in mind:

Quality Assurance: Even though AI can produce content quickly, it's still up to us to keep professional standards high. Check and improve AI-created content to make sure it meets your professional standards.

Attribution and Honesty: When AI is an important part of your work, be open about it when it's appropriate. This builds trust and sets clear expectations.

Human Judgement: Use AI tools to inform your decisions, not to decide for you. Your experience and understanding of situations are very important.

Managing Everyday Ethical Situations

Professional Communications: When using AI to communicate with clients or stakeholders, make sure the message is genuine and appropriate. AI can assist in writing, but the final message should show your professional tone of voice and understanding of the relationship.

Working Together as a Team: When using AI tools in teams, think about how they impact your colleagues' work and well-being. Make sure everyone knows how and why AI tools are being used.

Making Good Ethical Decisions

When using AI tools, you'll have to decide the best ways to use them. Your judgement is very important. Think about the work you're doing and how AI fits into it. Ask yourself if using AI tools helps you keep the quality your work needs. Your knowledge and experience in your area help you make these choices.

Think about everyone who is part of your work. Your colleagues might be impacted by your use of AI tools. Your clients rely on you to provide good work, no matter what tools you use. Other people rely on your expertise. Think about how your decisions to use AI tools could affect all of these relationships.

It's important to stay involved and aware when using AI tools. Different situations need different levels of evaluation. A quick email may only need a simple check, while an important report needs a more thorough review. Trust your experience to help you decide how much guidance each task needs.

Creating Trust with AI Tools

Using AI tools well means being fully responsible for what you do. When you write reports, look at data, or create presentations, the end result shows your professional quality. The AI can help with tasks, but your knowledge and experience make sure the work is done well.

When you're working with others, be open to how you used AI tools to help with your work. As we have gone through, AI can help you create initial content or look at data faster. Focus on how these tools can help you achieve better results instead of the technology behind them. This shows that you are using AI carefully to improve your work.

Make sure that using AI tools helps you reach your work goals. As you use these tools more, you'll get a clearer idea of when and how to use them effectively. Taking time to think about your work helps you change how you use AI, making sure it really helps you and keeps your professional standards high.

Remember that building trust takes time. Your careful use of AI tools, along with clear communication and high standards, builds trust in your approach.

Looking Forward

As AI grows, keeping ethical standards in mind is more important than ever. Use these tools to make your work even better and maintain the highest professional standards instead of harming them.

Consider this: How can you make sure that using AI tools builds trust in your professional relationships instead of weakening it?

In Chapter 8, we'll look at how to plan and implement AI projects successfully while keeping these ethical principles in mind.

Chapter Eight

Getting Started with AI Projects

Planning Your AI Journey

Now that we understand how to use AI tools in a responsible way, let's look at how we can apply these skills to make real improvements at work. Whether you run a small business, work in a trade, or are a professional in an organisation, having a clear plan makes all the difference.

Starting Your AI Project

Starting to use AI tools in your work is like learning to use any new tool. A carpenter wouldn't try a complicated joint without first learning the basic cuts. A chef wouldn't attempt a complicated recipe without knowing simple cooking methods. AI tools are similar—start with the basics and then build from there.

Finding the Best Starting Point

Sometimes, the best place to start isn't always the biggest problem. Start with something important that won't lead to or cause any major issues if it doesn't go to plan straight away.

A hairdresser might use AI to create aftercare instructions for clients before moving on to appointment scheduling. A plumber could start by using AI to make simple parts lists rather than full job quotes. In an office, you might start with one part of a report instead of the whole document.

When you're choosing your first AI project, think about tasks that:

- Take a lot of time but are not very complicated

- Come up often

- Take your time, slowing down other tasks

- Are important but not super critical (especially for your first project)

Setting Clear Goals

Rather than thinking in general about using AI in your work, focus on specific improvements you want to achieve. Think about clear goals that will really make a difference to your everyday tasks.

Here's how to make your goals clearer:

Instead of Saying	Try This Instead
Restaurant Owner: "Make ordering easier."	"Cut stock counting time by half."
Electrician: "Get better at paperwork."	"Create job quotes 30% faster."
Office Manager: "Have better customer service."	"Answer routine emails in less than an hour."
Retail Worker: "More efficient stock control."	"Cut stock-take time by two hours."

Planning Your Project

Think about your AI project the way that you plan for any other job. Whether you're planning a construction project, getting ready for a busy service, or organising an office move, It's important to understand what you're starting with, what tools are needed, and how you will know if it was successful.

A mechanic might need to write down how they currently diagnose vehicle issues before using AI to make the process faster. A chef may keep track of how long it takes to plan the menu before using AI to help with adjusting recipes. Someone in an office might check how much time it takes to write reports before using AI tools to help them.

Making It Happen

Start with small steps and build up gradually. A builder wouldn't start a full house renovation without trying out different techniques on smaller projects first. A restaurant wouldn't change its whole menu without testing new dishes as specials. This also applies for AI projects.

Here's how you could do it:

- Start with one straightforward process or task.

- Test out your approach with a small group first.

- Get feedback and make changes as you go.

- Grow slowly as you understand and see what's actually working well for you.

Helping People Adjust

Training a new apprentice, graduate, or helping more experienced staff learn new systems takes time and patience. A head chef understands that new kitchen procedures take time to become normal practice. A construction site supervisor knows that new safety protocols need simple explanations and practice for teams to understand them.

Make sure you have open communication about AI by:

- Clearly explaining the benefits.

- Listening to concerns and questions.

- Giving regular updates.

- Sharing relevant success

- stories.

Knowing If It's Working

Success is about getting things done and seeing the practical results. A florist might see that customer quotes take just a few minutes instead of a few hours. A dental practice might find that scheduling appointments gets easier. A warehouse worker might notice that stock checks are getting quicker and more accurate.

Keeping It Going

Think about ways to keep improving over time. Your AI processes need regular attention to stay effective, just like a restaurant keeps its food quality standards up or a construction site follows safety rules. You need to keep it going.

Looking Ahead

Keep in mind that successful AI projects aren't about making huge changes overnight. They're about finding practical ways to improve your work, step by step. Remember, work smart, not hard. Think about a regular task in your job that takes longer than it needs to—that could be a great place to start.

Next, we'll look at how to tell if your AI project is really making a difference to your work and what steps you can take to keep improving. We'll look at practical ways to gather feedback and make changes that help you get the most from your AI tools.

***

Taking AI from Idea to Action

After starting your AI project, you'll want to know if it's really making things better. Success is like a tailor making clothes adjustments for the perfect fit or a personal trainer changing a workout plan. More likely than not, success often calls for you to increasingly look at results and make careful changes with the goal of improving.

Understanding What Success Looks Like

Success means different things in different work environments. A gardener might find that they can spend less time on paperwork and more time with clients. A dentist receptionist might be able to schedule appointments faster and with fewer booking conflicts. In an office, it could mean making reports in half the usual time.

Think about what really matters in your job. A physiotherapist might prioritise having more time to focus on their patients. A builder might concentrate on making better material estimates. An office manager may want to manage everyday emails in a more efficient way.

Measuring Improvements

Here are some practical ways to keep track of your progress. Think of it like a weight loss journey—you wouldn't just assume that your new routine is simply working. You would likely be tracking your new routine, be it going to the gym or eating differently to how you did before. Look for obvious signs of progress.

Here are some ways to measure success:

Saving Time:
Keep track of the time it takes to complete tasks before and after using AI tools. A hairdresser may notice that the multiple client communications that they

used to send now take 25 minutes instead of an hour. An accountant might be able to finish basic reports in 30 minutes instead of taking two hours.

Quality Improvements:
Aim for better outcomes. A mechanic might see better parts orders without mistakes. A teacher might have clearer lesson plans. A marketing professional may need to now make fewer changes to draft content compared to what they did previously.

Getting Feedback

Getting clear and honest feedback about your AI project helps you see what's really making a difference. Sometimes the responses can catch you off guard—like finding out that your new coffee-making method is why everyone suddenly likes tea instead. These surprises help us grow and improve.

Your colleagues who are using the new tools will have helpful information to share. They may let you know how certain features help them do their job better or highlight parts where the old way worked better. Customers who notice changes in your service can also share by giving a different perspective on what's important to them. Make sure you listen to anyone else affected by the new processes; they can often notice important details that others might miss.

Changing How You Do Things

It's completely normal for things not to always work perfectly or go to plan straight away. Learning to ride a bike can be a bit shaky at first, but those early wobbles are just part of the process. Don't let them discourage you. You just need to change your balance a little.

You might see some signs that tell you that changes would be helpful. Some tasks might be taking more time than before. Some colleagues might be staying away from the new tools and prefer to use the methods they already know and are familiar with. Sometimes, unexpected surprises happen that no one saw coming. Or maybe the quality of work isn't quite up to your usual high standards. These are not failures; they are helpful hints about what needs focus and attention.

Improving How Things Work

Small changes can lead to surprisingly big results. Just like a chef understands that small changes in seasonings can change a dish, making slight tweaks in how you use AI tools can improve your results a lot. Different professionals usually find their own ways to make AI work better for their specific needs.

For example, service professionals might find that using AI to make quote templates can save them a lot of time each week instead of writing everything from scratch. Retail managers often find that AI is good at predicting stock needs, but it needs more guidance when it comes to communicating with customers. Property professionals might find that AI can help in creating property descriptions, but it's important to double-check when looking at market trends.

Learning from Experience

Every project teaches you something important, even if things don't turn out as you maybe planned. It's like learning a new skill. Every time you try, it helps you improve your understanding of what works best for you and your team.

You'll learn which tasks benefit the most from AI help and which ones need your personal touch. You'll get better at explaining changes to others in a way that makes sense to them. You will get better at knowing when to change your approach. You'll gain a better understanding of where human abilities are more important.

These lessons help you gain knowledge, helping you to make better choices about using AI tools in the future. Remember that the aim isn't to be perfect—it's about finding ways to work better while keeping the quality that your work demands.

What matters most is being open to learning and ready to change your approach based on what works in the real world. The best AI projects come from knowing what the technology can do and understanding the human aspects that make work important.

Consider your own AI project, if you have already undertaken one or are in the process—what lessons have you discovered that caught you off guard? What small changes might make a big difference in how well AI works?

Celebrating Progress

Don't forget to acknowledge improvements, no matter how small. Your AI-assisted email responses might not be perfect yet, but if they have improved since last week, that's something to recognise and celebrate. Success often comes in small steps rather than giant leaps.

Sharing What Works Best

If you find something useful, let others know so they can also benefit. A beautician might share effective appointment reminder templates with colleagues. A carpenter might help other trades in making their quoting processes better. Someone in an office could show colleagues how to do everyday tasks in a better way.

Looking Forward

As you get used to AI tools, you'll begin to get a sense of what works best for you. Just like any tool, AI is more useful when you learn how to use it well.

Consider this: What small win would give you confidence that your AI project is heading in the right direction?

In Chapter 9, we will look at how to bring together different AI tools to make your work easier.

Part 4: Advancing Your AI Journey

Chapter Nine

Making the Most of Your AI Tools

Making Your AI Tools Work as a Team

Using one AI tool well can improve your work. But knowing how to combine different AI tools can make an even bigger difference. This chapter looks at how to use multiple AI tools together in a smart way.

Why Think About Using Different Tools

A carpenter has many tools for many jobs. In the same way, each AI tool has strengths. ChatGPT can help with first drafts, whereas Claude can do more detailed work, such as analysis. Google Gemini provides current information, while Microsoft Copilot works smoothly with office documents (Word, PowerPoint, etc.). Knowing these different strengths helps you pick the best tools for your work.

Choosing to use multiple tools usually happens because one tool by itself may not be able to handle all the different parts of your work well. If you're creating a market report, you'll need up-to-date information, clear writing, and detailed analysis. No single tool does all these tasks perfectly.

It's important to know which tool to use at the right time. Just like you wouldn't grab a sledgehammer to hang a picture frame, you shouldn't use a complicated analysis tool for a simple draft email. It's important to choose the right tool for each part of your job.

Think about what you want to accomplish. Do you want fast first drafts that you can improve later? Do you need a clear look at complicated information? Got a bunch of data that needs to be formatted perfectly? These questions will help you choose the right selection of tools for the job.

Understanding Tool Combinations

Different AI tools can work well together in specific ways. Here are some combinations that may be useful:

AI Tool Combination	What It Offers	When To Use It
ChatGPT + Claude	Quick initial drafts with detailed review.	Complex documents that need thorough checking.
Google Gemini + Microsoft Copilot	Current information in correct format.	Reports requiring up-to-date data.
ChatGPT + Specialised Tools	General content with specific enhancements.	Projects needing both broad and deep expertise

Let's take a look at how these tool combinations work practically. You might start by using ChatGPT to create a first draft and then use Claude to help refine and make the draft better. This combination is good for important documents.

The combination of Google Gemini and Microsoft Copilot is helpful when you're dealing with the most up-to-date information that must match specific formats. Google Gemini can collect and summarise current information, while Microsoft Copilot helps in organising it neatly in your documents.

Using ChatGPT with more specialised tools lets you mix general skills with specific expertise of such a tool. You can use ChatGPT to help organise your content and then use specific tools to include technical details or specialised information. For example, a small business owner might use ChatGPT to create a draft of their social media content calendar but then use Canva to create the visuals of those posts. This way, they get AI help with planning and writing while using a specialised tool that makes their social media look professional and on-brand.

How to Create Your Approach

Using multiple AI tools for the first time needs some careful thinking and planning. Start by reviewing the way you typically work. Where do you spend the most time? What tasks need the most attention to detail? Which ones come up the most and never seem to go away? Knowing how you work can help you see where different tools could fit.

Think about your regular everyday tasks and how they can be divided into smaller steps. A report usually includes collecting information, arranging it, writing various parts, and doing the final edits. Different AI tools can work together to help with each of these steps.

The aim is to build a process that's easy and helps you work better, making things simpler, not harder. Start with one or two tools that work well together before you start adding more. This will help you see how they work together before you add more and start making things a little bit more complicated.

Getting Tools to Work Together

When you're using different AI tools together, there are some important things to pay attention to:

How Information Flows

Think about moving data between the different tools you use as you move from one tool to another. You may need to take some action, such as changing the format or layout of your work. This is because not all tools are necessarily the same. Make sure to write down where you put information and how you used it. This keeps things organised and makes sure nothing gets lost between tools.

Quality Guidelines

Define what you expect from each tool clearly. Understand which tool to use for different types of checks and reviews. One tool might be great for checking facts and numbers, while another might do a better job of improving the writing style and tone. Clear quality guidelines help in getting consistent results.

Managing Your Time

Plan how you'll use each tool. Spending extra time with one tool at the beginning can help you save time down the road. Sometimes, using multiple tools for quick checks is more effective. As you get to know how the tools work together, your way of managing time may change.

Dealing with Common Issues

Using many AI tools comes with certain challenges that you'll need to manage:

Consistency Between Tools

Different tools might give different answers to the same question. This is usual but needs to be managed. Find the tool you trust the most for certain things. Make straightforward rules about which tool's results are most important for different tasks. Make sure to keep track of which tool gave you what information. This way it's all clear.

Managing Information

Using multiple tools means dealing with more information. Create a simple system for:

- Keeping track of the tool you used for each task.

- Noting down tool combinations that work very well together.

- Writing down successful processes.

- Keeping an eye on any problems that come up.

Creating Effective Workflows

A good workflow with lots of AI tools will make your work easier and improve your results. Start by identifying your day-to-day tasks. Then think about how the different AI tools can help you. Some tasks may need only one tool, while others can be improved by using multiple tools together.

Start With Current Processes

Take a look at how you currently work. What steps do you take? Where do you spend the most time? Where do mistakes usually happen? Knowing how your current process works will help you see where AI tools can help in making the biggest difference.

Choose the Right Tools for the Job

Choose tools based on the needs of each part of your work. You might be interested in the following:

- A tool for coming up with ideas or first drafts.

- A second tool for reviewing and improving content.

- A third tool for final formatting or specific checks.

Test and Improve

Start with a low-risk task to try out your new workflow. Look at what is working well and what needs changing. Change things based on what you learn. Keep in mind that it could take a lot of trial and error to find the right combination of tools.

Making AI Tools Work Well Together

When you use multiple AI tools, it's really important to pay attention to quality. Like cooking with different ingredients, you want to make sure they all mix together nicely to make what you want.

Reviewing Your Work

Start by taking a quick look at your work. Are all the different tools being used working well together? Make sure the formatting and structure are the same and that you have what you want and expect.

Once you're happy with the basics, take a look at the details a little more closely. Make sure things like the writing style and tone of voice are delivered as you need and that the information is current. Think about how well different parts of your work fit together. Think about whether the end result is what you wanted. This deeper review helps make sure your work maintains your high professional standards.

Keeping Things Running Smoothly

Getting different AI tools to work together is like working on any good system—it needs regular attention to keep everything running smoothly. Every few weeks, take a moment to think about how your tools are working together:

- Are you still getting the results you want and need?

- Is your process still working well?

- Have your work needs changed lately?

- Can any new features make your work better?

Keep an eye on AI tool improvements, but don't let every update give you a headache. Look at the changes that can make your tasks better or improve your work. There might be a new feature that can help your tools work better together, or there could be a simpler way to use the tools you already have.

Remember that the aim isn't to use every tool and feature that's available. The goal is to find tool combinations that improve your work, making it better and easier. Keep what works well, change what could improve, and feel free to make changes when you have to. Stay agile.

Think about your own tasks—how might your AI tools work together more effectively to help you get more done?

Looking Ahead

As you get used to using multiple AI tools, you'll get a better sense of which ones work well together for different situations. Don't forget that the aim is not to use as many tools as possible but to find the right combinations that make your work better.

Think about the following questions:

- Which parts of your work might benefit most from combining different AI tools?

- Where could using multiple tools together have the biggest difference?

- What new tool combinations could you experiment with and try?

Moving Forward

Success using multiple AI tools is about finding the right balance. You want to use enough tools to improve your work without making it too complicated. Start with the basics, build your confidence, and change your approach as you learn what works best for your needs.

Next, we'll look at how to use AI to work faster without sacrificing quality.

***

Making AI Part of Your Daily Work

Now that we understand how various AI tools can work together, let's look at how to create smooth processes that save you time and maintain high-quality work. Think about this as creating your own guide for working well with AI, helping you along the way.

Getting Started with the Basics

A good work process does more than just make sure tasks end up getting completed—it helps you work smarter. Start by choosing a regular task you do a lot, like writing the weekly reports, putting together quotes, answering customer enquiries, or making presentations. Think about how AI might assist at each step.

If you take writing a report as an example, you could start by using Google Gemini to collect current information and then let ChatGPT help you organise all the key points. You can write your first draft faster with AI help, from the information provided and summarised, and then use Claude to help you polish up the content. The final step would be for you to review the report and add your personal professional touch to the final version.

Finding the Right Balance

For you to work well with AI, it's important to find a balance between using the tools and keeping your own professional control. You want to save time while still keeping quality high at the same time. Think about which tasks AI can manage well, and which ones need your skills.

Find ways that AI can make things faster, like helping with first drafts or checking the formatting. Focus on the regular tasks that take time but don't need a lot of creative thinking. Make sure you are always checking things at every step and stage, and decide which results or parts need your attention to detail and which can be checked by AI. Never forget that you are still in charge and responsible for making sure the work you present meets the professional standards that you set and are expected.

Creating Flexible Approaches

Your work process should change with the situation and not stay the same, unless they are working, of course. Sometimes, you might need to do things fast, and at other times, you might need to be extra careful and check through things. Here are some scenarios that usually work well for different tasks:

For Creating Content:

- Generate ideas and outlines with the help of AI.

- Use AI help you create your first draft.

- Use AI to improve your work and polish it up.

- Add your personal and professional touch in the final review.

For Analysis Work:

Use AI to collect and organise the generated information, then review the main points and trends yourself. AI can help explain the results but always check conclusions carefully by using your own professional judgement.

For Communication:

Start by creating your first messages with AI help, then change the style, tone of voice, and any other details to fit what you want. Make sure you check everything and that it all makes sense, and add your personal touch to the final version.

Making Things Run Smoothly

When your basic process is up and running, try to find ways to make it even better. Check if you're doing anything you don't need to—could some steps be combined? Can AI take care of more of the everyday tasks? Try to catch any problems early rather than later.

If you find steps that aren't working well, save them for next time. This might include helpful AI prompts, simple checking processes, or useful tool combinations.

Dealing with Obstacles

Every work process has its ups and downs. If quality drops, look at where things may be going wrong and change the way you are checking things. If tasks are taking too long, check for delays and see if some steps can be simplified. If the results are not the same each time, check how you're using each tool and make sure your instructions are clear.

Keeping Things Working Well

A good work process should keep delivering results over time. Every few months, make sure that your approach is still working well for you. Ask yourself if the process is still saving time and that the quality of what is being produced is high. Be ready to change things when tools have new features or when your work requirements change.

Let's look at how this could make an everyday task like writing a business update better. Instead of collecting the information manually, writing everything from scratch, and checking everything on your own, you could:

- Use AI to collect and summarise the key information.

- Make a fast first draft with the help of AI.

- Let AI help with checking and making any improvements.

- Review the key points yourself.

- Use AI to help with the final formatting.

This new approach could cut your work time in half while keeping or even improving the quality.

Good work processes evolve and improve as you learn what works best. Continue to explore different approaches and make changes based on what you learn. The goal is to improve your work and make it simpler, rather than using AI just for the sake of it.

Think about your own job—which everyday tasks could benefit the most with a better process? What little changes could make a big difference?

In Chapter 10, we will look at how AI is getting better and what new opportunities this could bring for making our work easier.

Chapter Ten

Growing with AI

What's New in AI Tools

AI is constantly evolving to help us work better. A recent development that stands out is something called AI agents. Think of an AI agent as a better version of the AI tools we've been talking about. It's like upgrading from a simple helper to a more skilled assistant that can manage lots of different tasks all at once.

Learning about AI Agents

Regular AI tools can help with specific tasks when you ask them, doing them one at a time, but AI agents can handle a series of tasks on their own. The difference is like asking someone to "write an email" compared to asking them to "manage my inbox." An AI agent can understand the overall situation and manage lots of tasks on its own without needing constant help.

For example, an AI tool can help you write one email. An AI agent can help you manage whole email communication by writing replies, suggesting follow-ups, remembering important details from previous email conversations, and high-lighting messages that need your personal attention.

How AI Agents Help in Real Work

The capabilities of AI agents are already having an impact in different work environments. Tale the daily tasks of a restaurant owner. An AI agent can help keep track of inventory levels, monitor upcoming bookings, and suggest staff rota's, all while understanding how these different parts of the business are connected.

An AI agent can help a salesperson keep in touch with lots of clients. It keeps track of and remembers past conversations, reminds you when you should follow up, and helps you get ready for meetings by collecting important relevant information about each client's history, likes, and dislikes. It's like having a helpful helper who keeps everything neat and organised.

Estate agents might find AI agents helpful for handling many property listings. The AI agent can help keep property details up to date on different platforms, e .g., Rightmove, arrange viewings while taking travel time into account, and help with tracking follow-ups with potential buyers, all while highlighting anything that desperately needs your personal attention.

What 's Possible Right Now

Today's AI agents are great at managing tasks and following step-by-step instructions. They can help organise and update information and find and summarise important details. They can also handle simple communications. They keep track of previous conversations, which makes them even more useful as time goes on.

As good as this all sounds, they still need your guidance. Think of them as useful helpers instead of self-sufficient workers. They are tools designed to help you in your work, not replace your own personal judgement and expertise.

Getting Started Safely

If you want to try AI agents, start with everyday tasks that have clear steps, similar to the advice on starting with regular AI tools. Choose tasks that give straightforward results instead of anything too complicated and where small mistakes won't lead to any major problems. You could start by managing follow-ups or organising information for your regular reports.

It's important to start with one simple task that you know inside out. This makes it easier to see if anything needs changing. Once you get comfortable, you can slowly start to look into more complex tasks.

Making Smart Choices

When you're thinking about where to use AI agents in your job, think about these questions:

- Is this task part of a usual pattern?

- Are mistakes easy to find, and correct?

- Can this really help me save time?

- How much checking is needed?

Start with tasks where making small mistakes won't lead to big problems. This allows you to learn and change things without getting stressed out.

Looking Forward

AI agents will keep improving, getting better at understanding situations and managing much more complicated tasks. But the main idea stays the same: they are tools to help you in working more effectively, not to replace your expertise.

Your personal experience and judgement become even more important as these tools start to handle the more basic tasks.

Think about the usual tasks in your job that have lots of steps. Where could an AI agent make the biggest difference to your efficiency? What routine tasks can you start to simplify first? Remember that the aim isn't to rely completely on AI. The aim is to find ways to work smarter and be more efficient while keeping the quality and personal touch that make your work important.

In the next section, we will look at other developments in AI tools and what these changes could mean for your work.

***

What's Coming Next

The world of AI is constantly moving forward, bringing new ways to improve the way we work. Let's look at what's coming up and what it could mean for your work life, focusing on useful changes instead of future predictions.

Getting to Know Tomorrow's Tools

AI tools are getting better at understanding and assisting us in our tasks. One of the most exciting developments is their improving ability to understand context. It can be very annoying to keep explaining the same background information to a new colleague or person we have just met. Future AI tools will be improved at remembering previous conversations and understanding the overall goals you want to achieve.

These tools are getting better at handling different types of information at the same time. Soon, you might be able to show an AI tool a view of your project, tell it what you need, and get helpful relevant suggestions that take into account both the project view and what you said to it. A designer might show an AI tool a photo of a room, explain what the client likes and dislikes, and get ideas that fit the space and the client's needs.

These things are already happening if you review some of the available tools at the time of publishing.

Making Work Flow Better

One of the most useful changes is that AI tools will be able to work together more smoothly. Rather than using different tools for different jobs, you could have one smooth experience where your calendar, email, and work tools all work well together. This means spending less time on tools and more time on important work.

What This Means for Different Professionals

These developments will impact different roles in different ways. If you work in customer service, AI tools could help you understand what customers need better. They suggest solutions based on what has worked well before, meaning you can focus on building real connections with people.

If you work in project management, future tools might help you spot possible problems before they happen. They might suggest changes based on patterns from past projects, but you'll still make the important decisions yourself.

Small business owners might find that AI tools can help them understand market trends and customer preferences. This can make it simpler to plan inventory and staffing while keeping the personal touch that makes their business unique.

Keeping the Human Touch

As these tools get better, your ability to make decisions becomes even more important. Being able to understand people, read situations well, and make thoughtful decisions will help skilled professionals stand out. The aim is not to rely completely on AI but to use it to improve your skills and expertise.

Think about how a skilled chef uses kitchen tools. The tools help with getting food ready as well as preparation and cooking timing, but it's the chef's knowledge and creativity that make the meal special. In the same way, future AI tools will take care of everyday tasks better, meaning you can focus on the parts of your job that need human understanding.

Getting Ready Without Stress

Being prepared for these changes doesn't mean you have to follow every new development all the time. Instead, focus on understanding the changes that could genuinely help your work. Use what you know about your current tools, as this helps you understand and then use the new features when they come out.

Start by thinking about which parts of your job could improve with AI tools that better understand context and manage complicated tasks better. How can these tool improvements help you in being able to give better service or value to your customers or colleagues?

Looking Forward

The future of AI in the workplace is not about taking over human expertise - it's about making it better. As these tools get better, they will help cut down on everyday tasks and give you more time to work on things that need your professional expertise and personal touch.

Think about your own work. Which parts would benefit from AI tools that understand your needs and work well together? How can you use these abilities to focus more on the parts of your job that you find most important?

In Chapter 11, we'll look at how to develop your career by using these changing capabilities, both today and in the future.

NOTE: It's important to remember that the AI landscape is constantly evolving. New tools and technologies are emerging all the time, and what was cutting-edge yesterday may be outdated tomorrow. As you explore the world of AI, keep an eye on the latest developments and be open to trying new things.

Chapter Eleven

Building Your Career with AI

Planning Your Professional Growth

As AI tools become more common and are used more often in many workplaces, you have chances to grow your career by learning how these tools can improve your professional skills. It's important to bring together your expertise with what AI can do. With all of this, you need to make sure that you are constantly delivering value.

Using Your Skills Effectively

Your professional expertise is the fundamental base of your career. When you know your field well and see how AI tools can help, you open up chances for further growth. In customer service, you could use AI to handle the more common questions, meaning you can spend more time focusing on building strong customer relationships. In project management, AI can help with scheduling and tracking a project so you can focus on leading your team better.

Making a Plan for Your Development

A clear plan for your career development helps you grow comfortably with AI tools. Start by focusing on the next few months of your journey. Use AI tools for simple work tasks, focusing on the areas where they can help the most. Take small steps and build up your confidence as you progress.

As you look at where you are from a time-of-year perspective, think about how AI tools could improve your work processes. You might find ways to handle complicated projects better by using your expertise with AI tools. It's always a good time to develop the skills you have that work well with AI, including critical thinking and problem-solving. Think about sharing your knowledge with colleagues, as helping others will also help yourself.

As you think about the next few years, look for roles where your skills and understanding of AI can create new value. You might find chances to manage AI projects or create new solutions that combine human expertise with AI. Think about how your industry might evolve and find ways to contribute in that future.

Building Important Skills

As AI becomes part of everyday work, some skills are becoming more important. Critical thinking helps you check AI suggestions and see when something needs human attention. Good communication skills help you to explain ideas clearly and build trust with customers and colleagues.

Problem-solving becomes more important when you see how AI can help and manage situations that are not normal. These skills help you keep quality high while using AI tools well. Your ability to identify what works in real-life situations is very important. AI can give you information and suggestions, but understanding how to use that information needs human expertise.

Making Chances for Growth

When your workplace starts using AI tools, find ways to help with their implementation. Your understanding of the work you do and how AI tools can help is very important. Think about ways to make things better—maybe customer service could feel more personal, or quality checks could be done more carefully.

Helping your colleagues learn how to use AI tools helps develop your leadership skills. Helping others not only supports your team but also increases your own understanding of how to use these tools well.

Keeping an Eye on Your Progress

Make sure you keep notes about your journey with AI tools. Experiment with different approaches and keep track of what's working well. Learn from situations that don't go to plan; they usually give you the most valuable insights. Share your experiences with colleagues to help everyone improve.

Keep a record of the improvements that you make. Keep track of the time saved and the improvements in quality. Get feedback that shows the actual benefits of your growing skills from using AI tools. Keep up to date with any changes in your specific area but concentrate on the skills that can really benefit your work instead of trying to keep track of every new trending AI development.

Building Long-term Value

When AI takes care of everyday tasks, you have more time to learn new skills and work on more exciting projects. Using AI tools shows that you are thinking ahead and have the potential to lead. Bringing together what you know about your job with an understanding of AI opens up new opportunities for growth.

Remember that developing your career with AI can be done step by step and doesn't need to happen all at once. Taking small, consistent steps to learn and use AI tools can result in big improvements over time. Keep doing a good job in your current role while slowly learning new skills.

Think about what you want to do next. What small step can you take this week to improve your professional growth using AI?

In the next section, we'll look at ways to help others succeed with AI tools, whether you are a leader or someone who supports your colleagues.

***

Helping Others Succeed with AI

If you're a team leader or someone who likes seeing their colleagues improve, knowing how to help others in using AI tools well is becoming a very useful skill. Success happens when we assist people in keeping professional standards and discovering better ways to work.

Guiding with Experience

Leading in a workplace with AI isn't about being a tech expert. It's about helping people to use AI tools well while keeping professional standards high. Your experience in understanding what makes work successful is even more useful when helping others.

Think about a restaurant manager who understands that customer satisfaction depends on more than just quick service. When they're helping their team with AI tools for bookings or stock take, they make sure everyone keeps the personal touch that brings customers back. They focus on combining the usefulness of AI with the kindness of people. The human touch.

Supporting Your Team

Different team members will use AI tools with different levels of confidence. Some people may want to jump in and try everything, while others like to take things slowly. Good guidance means understanding and dealing with these differences.

A construction supervisor might help their team in using AI for project planning and also make sure that everyone follows important safety and quality standards. They understand that AI tools are meant to support any professional judgement, not replace it. An office manager helping their team in using AI for document handling makes sure everyone knows how important it is to be accurate and confidential when dealing with client files and information.

Creating an Environment for Success

People learn best when they feel supported and motivated. Creating this type of environment means recognising that everyone learns at their own pace and making sure no one ever feels left behind. A retail team leader might start by asking the more confident team members to use AI tools for managing stock. They can then share what they learnt with the rest of the team. Learning from each other can sometimes be more effective than giving formal instructions.

When you introduce new tools or processes, start with the tasks where mistakes are easy to notice and then fix. A payroll manager might start by using AI to check simple calculations before moving on to the more complicated tasks. This helps to slowly build confidence while making sure things are accurate.

Maintaining Quality

As teams start to use AI tools more often, keeping the quality of work high is becoming more important. Help your team to understand when to rely on AI suggestions and when to use their own professional experience. A GP practice manager makes sure that even though AI might help with scheduling appointments and managing records, their team still needs to pay close attention to the details that patients need.

Regular quality checks and open discussions about what works well will help everyone keep high standards. Encourage team members to talk about their wins and struggles; this helps build a culture of continuous improvement.

Handling Change Well

When we start new ways of working, it's normal to have questions and concerns. Pay attention to what team members say about how AI tools might impact their work. Be open about concerns and show people how these tools can improve their jobs instead of putting them at risk.

Make sure everyone understands how AI tools fit into your team's work. Give enough time and support for learning new approaches. Remember that change takes time; enjoy the little wins and see challenges as chances to learn.

Building Long-term Success

Look past the first steps of introducing AI to make a real and lasting difference. Think about how you can keep quality high as teams get more comfortable with AI tools. Find ways to share your knowledge as people develop different skills. Make sure your processes are up to date as capabilities improve.

Help team members grow by finding chances for them to learn new skills. Encourage people to share what they know, and don't forget to highlight the ones who take initiative in finding better ways to work.

Supporting Growth and Development

Good leaders support their teams in building their skills while using AI tools. Find opportunities for team members to learn new skills and take on extra responsibilities. Remember that helping others grow can lead to surprising new ideas that help everyone.

Think about setting up mentoring opportunities where you could pair up team members so they can help each other learn. This builds confidence and helps create a collaborative atmosphere where everyone plays a part in the team's success.

Looking Forward

Success in a workplace that utilises AI comes from getting the best out of people and making good use of the tools that are available. Help your team to focus on making sure they keep up their professional standards and also find better ways to work. Remember that your experience and understanding of what makes work successful are very important as you help others in dealing with these changes.

Think about your own workplace: What can you do to help others feel more confident about using AI tools well? What small step can you take to help someone on their learning journey?

This brings us to the appendices, which include some helpful resources to help you on your AI journey.

Appendix

Appendix A: Resources for Non-Technical Professionals

A1: Essential Tools and Platforms

This guide covers some of the key AI tools you're most likely to use in your professional work. The focus is on well-known, established platforms that have shown they are reliable and keep evolving based on user need. This is your practical starting point for working with AI.

General-Purpose AI Assistants

ChatGPT is probably the most well-known AI tool from OpenAI. It provides understanding and helpful responses based on user input. The free version offers good features for everyday tasks, while ChatGPT Plus and ChatGPT Pro, which are charged at different prices, provide more advanced features and priority access. ChatGPT is good at understanding context and keeps a level of consistency as conversations go.

ChatGPT is useful for drafting content, analysing information, and explaining complicated topics in simple terms. When checking information that has been given, make sure you always double-check important facts, especially for things that are in the moment and are time sensitive.

Claude 3, the latest version from Anthropic, is great at detailed analysis and handling complicated tasks. The platform is great at staying focused during much longer conversations and also at handling more complicated scenarios. From my experience, Claude 3 takes time to carefully think about problems and explains things in a nice, clear way. The free version has the basic features, but the paid version, known as Claude Pro, has the more advanced features, like increased usage limits, access to more powerful models, and their priority support.

Claude 3 is also great for thorough research projects and detailed professional analysis. Responses might take a bit longer to generate than some other tools, but the extra time is usually worth it for the detailed answers you get.

Google Gemini Advanced is a powerful AI tool that can find and understand the latest information. Just think Google. It's great for research and gives you detailed answers. Google Gemini (the free version) is a good starting point, but Gemini Advanced provides gives you a more advanced experience. The platform gives helpful context-aware responses and also gives you current information.

Google Gemini is very useful for research tasks and keeping up to date with industry-related developments. The main features are the same everywhere, even though some capabilities might change depending on your location.

Workplace Integration Tools

Microsoft Copilot Pro (paid version) is the latest version from Microsoft. It's a powerful AI tool that works seamlessly with Microsoft 365 applications like Word, Excel, PowerPoint, and Teams. It can assist you with everyday tasks and make your work more efficient. This is especially useful for those who already use Microsoft programs. Microsoft Copilot (the free version) is a good starting point, but Microsoft Copilot Pro provides a more advanced experience.

Microsoft Copilot stands out for its ability to improve your existing workflows without needing major changes to how you already work, especially if your business already uses the Microsoft 365 suite. Don't forget that you need a subscription and your company's approval.

Specialised Tools

Grammarly Business with AI Writing Assistant can do more than just spelling and grammar checks. It can help you write better by offering suggestions for tone, clarity, and overall effectiveness. This helps keep your writing the same and consistent, especially if you have a team or teams.

The free version of Grammarly is good for basic writing checks, but Grammarly Business has extra features. It can help you with building sentence structure, vocabulary, and style. It can check your work for plagiarism and also help you change the tone of your writing. If your business is looking to improve their writing quality and consistency, then Grammarly Business is worth taking a look at.

Canva is a handy design tool that helps you make great visuals, especially for non-designers. Canva allows you to create professional-looking designs for things like social media posts, presentations, and marketing materials. Canva's AI features mean you can generate ideas, create custom images, and improve your designs.

Canva has a free version, but their premium version gives you more advanced features like more templates, brand kits, and the ability to remove image backgrounds.

Getting Started

When choosing your first AI tool, think about your main job responsibilities and the most common tasks. What problem are you trying to solve? Lots of professionals start with either ChatGPT or Microsoft Copilot, based on what their workplace setup is. These platforms provide a lot of features and are easy for beginners to use.

Think about the tasks that take up most of your time and how AI might help. Also, make sure you check your organisation's rules about AI tools, as more companies start to have clear guidelines on how to choose and use them.

Safety and Access

Most AI platforms provide better security features in their paid for versions. Free versions give you generic features for basic needs, but professional versions usually come with extra privacy protections and security features that would be better for business use.

Don't forget to check your organisation's rules on using AI tools. Companies now have specific guidelines about which AI tools employees should use and how they should also manage sensitive information.

Moving Forward

Don't try to use every AI tool out there but find the right tools for your specific needs. Start with one tool that fits your daily tasks, and then as you get confident, add more tools as long as they meet your needs.

Remember that these tools are here to help you improve your skills and not to replace your knowledge. Using them for everyday tasks makes them most useful, allowing you to focus on work that needs human insight and decision-making.

This summary highlights just a few of the available tools. are constantly improving and are great options for those new to AI. There are many other tools out there, so take a look at others that might help with specific problems you come across at work.

***

A2: Learning Resources and Communities

Finding reliable resources and helpful communities can really help you in your AI learning journey. This guide shows a few sources of information and welcoming communities where you can learn and grow alongside others.

Online Learning Courses and Websites

AI for Everyone by DeepLearning.AI (Coursera): A practical course created for professionals without a technical background who want to get a better understanding of AI. It shows you how AI can make business operations better without getting into the complicated technical side. The course uses real examples and gives you practical experience using some popular AI tools.

Introduction to Artificial Intelligence by IBM (Coursera): This course simplifies AI concepts into clear and easy-to-understand modules. It's especially helpful for people who want to see how AI is changing the way businesses work. The course makes AI easy to understand and shows you how to apply it to real-life situations.

Generative AI for Everyone by DeepLearning.AI (Coursera): This course shows you the latest developments in AI, like ChatGPT and other similar tools. It explains how new AI tools can assist you in your work, with a lot of practical examples that make sense for business professionals.

Google AI Essentials (Coursera): Created for professionals who want to learn the basics of AI and how to use it responsibly. The program helps you understand how AI affects different industries and helps you think about the ethical side of things. This course is especially useful if you're looking to understand how AI fits into wider business situations.

Microsoft Learn's AI Business School (Microsoft). This free resource from Microsoft gives helpful tips for using AI in business. It's especially useful if you're part of the decision-making process regarding AI in your organisation. The courses use real business examples to show how AI can improve organisational strategy and operations.

Professional Communities

AI for Business Network: This Facebook group is a good place to learn about AI in a straightforward way. Get advice from other business owners who are using AI to improve their processes. If you're just starting out or want to know what's new in the industry, you'll find lots of helpful tips and information. Members talk about their experiences, ask questions, and discuss the challenges of using AI tools. The community has a friendly approach that makes it easy for newcomers to feel welcome.

LinkedIn AI Professionals Groups: There are lots of active LinkedIn AI groups of people using AI in their jobs. Discussions about new tools, best practices, and what's happening in the space are themes across a large number of these groups. Members frequently share helpful tips and personal stories. As mentioned, there are loads of groups around, so find ones that work for you.

Women in AI: A supportive group encouraging diversity in implementing and using AI. It provides chances for mentorship and hosts regular events to share knowledge. Very helpful for connecting with others and discovering role models in the field.

Online Forums and Chat Groups

r/AIforProfessionals on Reddit: A forum that is moderated and focuses on how AI can be used in business. Members talk about their experiences, ask questions, and share helpful tips. The community keeps things non-technical and easy to understand. There are many other subreddits you can explore.

AI Tools Learning and Discussion Group: An active Facebook group where people talk about different AI tools and how they can be used. The group focuses on making AI easy to understand and is good to learn about new tools and features.

Free Resources

AI Learning Hub: Is a website that has loads of free resources for people who want to learn about AI. They have things like guides, tutorials, hands-on projects, and case studies. Their content is regularly updated as things constantly change.

AI Tools Newsletters: You can sign up to lots of AI newsletters that send updates daily or weekly. Newsletters with different topics include AI tools updates, new developments, and features for businesses and professionals.

Getting Started

When you're looking at different resources:

- Start with one or two things that match your needs.

- Focus less on the complicated technical side of things.

- Connect with others who work in similar jobs or industries and are also learning.

- Share your own experiences as you learn.

Building Your Network

Think about joining a professional community and a discussion group to start. This mix means you get structured learning and opportunities for knowledge sharing. As you get more comfortable, you can increase your involvement according to what you like and need.

Staying Current

The AI field changes quickly, but you don't have to keep up with every single development. Instead:

- Focus on changes that matter to your work

- Learn from what others have gone through and are doing

- Share your own thoughts as you have them

- Build connections with people in your area of work

Remember that everyone starts somewhere at different points, and these groups are open to new members. Feel free to ask questions or look for help as you learn.

This overview shares some resources that I've found for people who want to learn how to use AI tools. The world of AI learning is huge and always changing. These suggestions are to help you on your way. They are just a starting point. There are hundreds or even thousands of courses, communities, and resources out there.

Use these suggestions to start your own journey. Everyone's got their own way of getting to where they want to or need to, and you might find that certain things work better for you. Think about joining different groups, trying out different learning platforms, and following experts who match your interests.

Remember that the best resources are most likely the ones you'll find when you do your own research. Don't limit yourself to these suggestions. Use them as a starting point to build your own collection of trusted resources and communities.

Appendix B: AI Tool Implementation Guide

B1: Tool Selection and Setup Guide

Choosing and using the right AI tools for your job can make a big difference in your success. This guide will help you pick, set up, and optimise AI tools that fit your work needs.

Understanding Your Requirements

Make sure you know what you need them for before choosing any AI tools. Think about the jobs you do often and where AI could be useful. Think about your usual workday—which things take up most of your time? What tasks are you repeating? Where do you usually need help?

For example, if you spend a lot of time writing reports and team updates, you may want to focus on tools that help you with writing and editing. If you work with data, choose tools that have good analysis features for that information. It's important to get the tools that fit your actual needs instead of just going for what's popular or has features you might never use.

Evaluating Tool Options

When you're looking at different AI tools, think about these factors:

Ease of Use: Think about how easy the tool is to use and if it works well with your routine. A strong tool that's hard to use may be less useful than a simpler one that fits easily into the way you work.

Integration Capabilities: Think about how the AI tool will fit in with what other tools in your organisation. Will it work well with the software you already use? If you mainly use Microsoft Office, a tool that works with these applications would likely be more useful than one that doesn't.

Safety Features: Understanding the security features of different tools helps you choose the right ones. Think about if the tool gives you what you need in terms of data protection, meeting any guidelines your organisation has set.

Tool Assessment Framework

When you're evaluating AI tools for your work, it's helpful to have a clear method to compare different options. This framework shows some important factors to think about, questions to ask for each factor, and their importance in your decision-making process. Use this guide when you're looking at potential tools, changing the priority levels to meet your specific needs.

Evaluation Factor	Questions to Consider	Priority Level
Main Functionality	Does it meet your primary needs?	High
Ease of Use	How hard is it to learn?	High
Integration	Does it work with tools you already have?	Medium
Security Features	Does it meet your security needs?	High
Cost vs. Value	Is it worth the cost?	Medium
Support Available	What support is available?	Medium

Signs of Successful Implementation

Once you start using your chosen AI tools, you'll want to see if they're actually improving your work. The following table shows important areas to keep an eye on, what to measure in each area, and simple ways to keep track of these measurements. This framework makes sure your AI tools are giving real benefits to your work. Think about keeping an eye on and tracking these indicators from the start of your implementation. This makes it easier to show the impact of your AI use.

Area	What to Measure	How to Track
Time Savings	Getting tasks done faster	Compare before / after times
Quality	Better quality results, outputs	Review accuracy and consistency
User Adoption	Team using the tool regularly	Monitor usage patterns
Work Impact	Impact on the overall efficiency	Track completed tasks and outcomes
Cost Efficiency	If the tool is worth the money spent on it	Compare costs against the benefits

Setting Up for Success

After you pick a tool, setting it up correctly is important for using it well. Start with the simple settings and slowly look into more advanced features as you get more comfortable.

Initial Setup

Start with the basics that will affect how you use the tool every day. Think about:

1. What language you'll work in and how you want the AI to communicate back with you. For instance, if you prefer direct, brief responses or more detailed explanations.

2. How you'll use the tool for regular tasks. If you write business emails often, you might set up your preferred professional writing style. This will make sure the AI understands how formal or casual you want its responses to be.

3. Any security settings your workplace needs you to have. Check with your company about any specific security guidelines that you need to follow.

4. Start with these basic settings before exploring more advanced features. This will help you build up your confidence before you move on to the more complicated features.

Improving Your Tools

This involves:

Customisation

Change the settings to fit how you work. When you use an AI writing tool, create templates for your more common documents or messages that you work with often. For analytical tools, setup report formats that fit your needs.

Learning Features

Spend some time to learn about the features that could improve your work. Many tools have features that can do more than what you might think at first. For instance, an AI writing assistant might have features for research or style checking that could improve your communications.

Making Workflows Work Well

Creating smooth workflows helps you make the best use of your AI tools. Think about how each tool works with your overall work process. Write down what works well and improve it using what you've learnt.

For example, you might create a workflow for making client proposals:

- Use AI to generate the initial draft content outline

- Use your expertise to make changes to the proposal

- Use AI tools to improve and refine the document

- Check and make the final changes

Monitoring and Changing

Frequent checks will help you make sure that your tools keep meeting your needs effectively. Pay attention to:

Performance

Keep an eye on how well the tool works on your daily tasks. Are the responses what you want and expected? Could you make some changes for the tool to work better?

Efficiency

You need to check if the tool actually helps you save time and effort. Making small changes in how you use a tool can sometimes improve how well it works.

Fixing Common Problems

Knowing how to deal with common problems helps keep tools from working well. This might include:

Connection Problems

Understand the simple steps to fix connectivity problems that could affect the performance of the tool.

Output Quality

Create plans to improve results when the tool doesn't meet your needs.

Looking Ahead

Keep up with updates and new features for the tools that you use. Many AI tools often add features or update existing ones that could improve your work. Make sure you set aside time to check how you're using your tools to make sure you're getting the most out of any new updates and features.

Remember that choosing and setting up tools is not something you just do once. Your needs may likely change over time, so you need to be adaptable. The goal is to find a set of tools that help to improve your skills; make sure they are easy to use and are effective.

Think about writing down your experiences with different tools. The knowledge you gain is useful when you help colleagues or change your methods as your work evolves.

The most successful professionals know that choosing and setting up AI tools is something they keep improving over time, not just a one-time thing. Be open and aware of how well your tools work for you and be ready to make changes if and when necessary.

***

B2: Making AI Tools Part of Your Work

Getting AI tools to work smoothly in your daily tasks needs some careful planning and a little bit of patience. This section looks at easy ways to include AI in your daily work routine while keeping quality and productivity high.

Starting with What Works

Before you make any changes to how you work, take a moment to understand your current routines. Think about how you manage your daily tasks and where AI tools might help you instead of messing up your current ways of working. When you first start using AI tools, choose one area where you are sure you will notice clear benefits. For instance, if you regularly write reports, start by using AI to help create the first drafts instead of changing your whole writing process all at once.

Understanding Your Journey

It's best to gradually introduce AI tools to your work. Everyone moves at their own speed, but having a basic timeline can help set realistic expectations. Like working backwards from what you want your end goal to be. This is a practical guide to help you in planning:

Stage	Duration	What to Focus On	What Success Looks Like
First Steps	Weeks 1-2	Setting up tools and trying simple tasks	Basic features working well
Early Days	Weeks 2-4	Using tools in your daily work	Using it regularly and confidently
Building Confidence	Months 2-3	Fine-tuning how you work	Work getting easier
Moving Forward	Month 4+	Looking at advanced features	Clear boosts in efficiency

Maintaining Quality

AI tools can help improve your work, but it's still very important to keep professional standards. A clear way for having quality checks helps you make sure results are the same every time. Here's a way to check your work:

Stage	What to Review	Key Actions	Expected Outcome
Initial Check	Basic accuracy	Quick review of content	Find obvious issues
Detailed Review	Professional standards	Check against requirements	Meet quality standards
Final Look	Overall effectiveness	Confirm final version	Ready to use
Follow-up	Results and impact	Write down what worked	Learn and improve

Getting Everything to Work Together

Your AI tools should easily blend in with how you already work. Think about your whole process, not just the parts where AI helps. For instance, if you use AI for talking to customers, think about how this fits with your usual way of handling customer relationships and following up with people.

Watch out for times when work moves from AI tools to human involvement. These points often need extra attention to make sure everything runs smoothly. For example, handling customer feedback at work. You might use an AI tool to help sort through and summarise all the customer comments, which will be the easy bit. But then your team needs to read these summaries and write back to the customers. This handover from AI to your team is a bit like passing a baton in a relay race—you need to make sure nothing gets dropped. Getting this handover right helps keep everything running smoothly and makes sure you don't miss anything important.

When you find processes that work well, make sure to write them down so you can use them again and again.

How to Manage Your Time

Be realistic and understand that learning new tools takes time. Tasks might take you a bit longer to get used to at first. Set aside some time to continuously check how things are going and make changes if they are needed. Don't keep doing the same thing if you don't think it's working or not having the desired effect. Many people find monthly reviews useful. It gives them enough time to see patterns and catch any problems early.

Working with Others

When you're using AI tools in a team, that means that clear communication is very important. Have some guidelines for how team members should keep track of how they're using AI tools. This keeps things consistent and makes it easier to sort out any problems that come up.

Make sure that helpful methods are shared with the team. When someone finds a good way to use an AI tool for a regular task, make sure others can learn and benefit from this success.

Making Sure Everything is Secure

Be aware of the security needs your company has while you're using AI tools. Make sure you know what information you can share with AI tools and follow your company's guidelines. Checking your security practices helps make sure you're using AI tools the right way.

Solving Common Problems

Create clear ways for dealing with common issues with AI tools. Know what to do when tools don't work as you maybe would have expected. Having these steps in place helps you stay productive, even when things get difficult. Write down any problems you face and how you fix them. This will help you and others avoid the same issues in the future.

Checking Progress

Make sure you are regularly checking how well the AI tools are working for you. Keep track of the changes and improvements that are important for your work, like time you've saved or better quality of work. Use this information to help you decide how to change your approach.

Looking Forward

Remember that using AI tools in your work is a continuous process. Keep up to date with updates and new features that might make your work easier and better. Check your approach often to make sure it still works well and meets your needs.

The best way to use AI tools is to find the right balance between their capabilities and your own professional judgement. Focus on finding ways that simplify your work instead of making it harder.

Think about your own work: How might you make AI tools naturally fit into your daily tasks without losing the quality that your work needs?